MznLnx

Missing Links Exam Preps

Exam Prep for

Basic Mathematical Skills with Geometry

Hutchison, Baratto, & Bergman, 7th Edition

The MznLnx Exam Prep is your link from the texbook and lecture to your exams.
The MznLnx Exam Preps are unauthorized and comprehensive reviews of your textbooks.

All material provided by MznLnx and Rico Publications (c) 2010
Textbook publishers and textbook authors do not particpate in or contribute to these reviews.

MznLnx

Rico
Publications

Exam Prep for Basic Mathematical Skills with Geometry
7th Edition
Hutchison, Baratto, & Bergman

Publisher: Raymond Houge
Assistant Editor: Michael Rouger
Text and Cover Designer: Lisa Buckner
Marketing Manager: Sara Swagger
Project Manager, Editorial Production: Jerry Emerson
Art Director: Vernon Lowerui

Product Manager: Dave Mason
Editorial Assitant: Rachel Guzmanji
Pedagogy: Debra Long
Cover Image: Jim Reed/Getty Images
Text and Cover Printer: City Printing, Inc.
Compositor: Media Mix, Inc.

(c) 2010 Rico Publications
ALL RIGHTS RESERVED. No part of this work covered by the copyright may be reproduced or used in any form or by an means--graphic, electronic, or mechanical, including photocopying, recording, taping, Web distribution, information storage, and retrieval systems, or in any other manner--without the written permission of the publisher.

Printed in the United States
ISBN:

For more information about our products, contact us at:
Dave.Mason@RicoPublications.com

For permission to use material from this text or product, submit a request online to:
Dave.Mason@RicoPublications.com

Contents

CHAPTER 1
Operations on Whole Numbers 1

CHAPTER 2
Multiplying and Dividing Fractions 17

CHAPTER 3
Adding and Subtracting Fractions 24

CHAPTER 4
Decimals 29

CHAPTER 5
Ratios and Proportions 38

CHAPTER 6
Percents 41

CHAPTER 7
Measurement 45

CHAPTER 8
Geometry 50

CHAPTER 9
Data Analysis and Statistics 62

CHAPTER 10
The Real Number System 69

CHAPTER 11
An Introduction to Algebra 79

ANSWER KEY 87

TO THE STUDENT

COMPREHENSIVE

The *MznLnx* Exam Prep series is designed to help you pass your exams. Editors at MznLnx review your textbooks and then prepare these practice exams to help you master the textbook material. Unlike study guides, workbooks, and practice tests provided by the texbook publisher and textbook authors, *MznLnx* gives you **all** of the material in each chapter in exam form, not just samples, so you can be sure to nail your exam.

MECHANICAL

The MznLnx Exam Prep series creates exams that will help you learn the subject matter as well as test you on your understanding. Each question is designed to help you master the concept. Just working through the exams, you gain an understanding of the subject--its a simple mechanical process that produces success.

INTEGRATED STUDY GUIDE AND REVIEW

MznLnx is not just a set of exams designed to test you, its also a comprehensive review of the subject content. Each exam question is also a review of the concept, making sure that you will get the answer correct without having to go to other sources of material. You learn as you go! Its the easiest way to pass an exam.

HUMOR

Studying can be tedious and dry. MznLnx's instructional design includes moderate humor within the exam questions on occassion, to break the tedium and revitalize the brain

Chapter 1. Operations on Whole Numbers

1. In mathematics, the _____ is a term used to describe the number of times one must apply a given operation to an integer before reaching a fixed point.

Usually, this refers to the additive or multiplicative persistence of an integer, which is how often one has to replace the number by the sum or product of its digits until one reaches a single digit. Because the numbers are broken down into their digits, the additive or multiplicative persistence depends on the radix.

   a. Linear congruence theorem
   b. Coprime
   c. Persistence of a number
   d. Lychrel number

2. _____ is simply the manner of writing out an expression in full. When a quantity is written as a sum of terms, or as a continued product, _____ notation is used to illustrate the expression in its entirety.
   a. Algebraic function
   b. Algebraic element
   c. Expanded form
   d. Algebra

3. In mathematics, a _____ is a set of numbers,, together with one or more operations, such as addition or multiplication.

Examples of _____s include: natural numbers, integers, rational numbers, algebraic numbers, real numbers, complex numbers, p-adic numbers, surreal numbers, and hyperreal numbers.

   a. Number system
   b. Slope
   c. Tally marks
   d. Number line

4. _____ is a special mathematical relationship between two quantities.Two quantities are called proportional if they vary in such a way that one of the quantities is a constant multiple of the other, or equivalently if they have a constant ratio.
   a. Proportionality
   b. Depth
   c. Compression
   d. Discontinuity

5. _____, also sometimes known as standard form or as exponential notation, is a way of writing numbers that accommodates values too large or small to be conveniently written in standard decimal notation. _____ has a number of useful properties and is often favored by scientists, mathematicians and engineers, who work with such numbers.

In _____, numbers are written in the form:

$$a \times 10^b$$

    a. 1-center problem
    b. Radix point
    c. Scientific notation
    d. Leading zero

6. In mathematics, the _____ of a real number is its numerical value without regard to its sign. So, for example, 3 is the _____ of both 3 and −3.

The _____ of a number a is denoted by $|a|$.

Generalizations of the _____ for real numbers occur in a wide variety of mathematical settings.

    a. A Mathematical Theory of Communication
    b. Absolute value
    c. A chemical equation
    d. Area hyperbolic functions

7. _____ is a numeral system in which each position is related to the next by a constant multiplier, a common ratio, called the base or radix of that numeral system.
    a. Cyrillic numerals
    b. NegaFibonacci coding
    c. Negative base
    d. Place value

8. In mathematics, a _____ can mean either an element of the set {1, 2, 3, ...} (i.e the positive integers) or an element of the set {0, 1, 2, 3, ...} (i.e. the non-negative integers).

a. Bounded
b. Degrees of freedom
c. Whole Number
d. FISH

9. In mathematics, a _____ can mean either an element of the set {1, 2, 3, ...} or an element of the set {0, 1, 2, 3, ...}. The latter is especially preferred in mathematical logic, set theory, and computer science.

_____s have two main purposes: they can be used for counting, and they can be used for ordering.

a. Cardinal numbers
b. Natural number
c. Suslin cardinal
d. Strong partition cardinal

10. A _____ number is a positive integer which has a positive divisor other than one or itself. By definition, every integer greater than one is either a prime number or a _____ number.zero and one are considered to be neither prime nor _____. For example, the integer 14 is a _____ number because it can be factored as 2 × 7.

a. Basis
b. Discontinuity
c. Key server
d. Composite

11. A _____ is a positive integer which has a positive divisor other than one or itself. In other words, if 0 < n is an integer and there are integers 1 < a, b < n such that n = a × b then n is composite. By definition, every integer greater than one is either a prime number or a _____.

a. Ruth-Aaron pair
b. Composite Number
c. Prime Pages
d. Megaprime

12. An _____ is a number which is involved in addition. A number being added is considered to be an _____.

a. Addend
b. A posteriori
c. A chemical equation
d. A Mathematical Theory of Communication

Chapter 1. Operations on Whole Numbers

13. In mathematics, a _____ is a picture of a straight line in which the integers are shown as specially-marked points evenly spaced on the line. Although this image only shows the integers from -9 to 9, the line includes all real numbers, continuing 'forever' in each direction. It is often used as an aid in teaching simple addition and subtraction, especially involving negative numbers.
    a. Number system
    b. Point plotting
    c. Real number
    d. Number line

14. In mathematics, the _____ of a Euclidean space is a special point, usually denoted by the letter O, used as a fixed point of reference for the geometry of the surrounding space. In a Cartesian coordinate system, the _____ is the point where the axes of the system intersect. In Euclidean geometry, the _____ may be chosen freely as any convenient point of reference.
    a. OMAC
    b. Autonomous system
    c. Interval
    d. Origin

15. In mathematics the _____ of a set which is equipped with the operation of addition is an element which, when added to any element x in the set, yields x. One of the most familiar additive identities is the number 0 from elementary mathematics, but additive identities occur in other mathematical structures where addition is defined, such as in groups and rings.

    - The _____ familiar from elementary mathematics is zero, denoted 0. For example,

    $5 + 0 = 5 = 0 + 5$.

    - In the natural numbers N and all of its supersets, the _____ is 0. Thus for any one of these numbers n,

    $n + 0 = n = 0 + n$.

    Let N be a set which is closed under the operation of addition, denoted +. An _____ for N is any element e such that for any element n in N,

    $e + n = n = n + e$.

    a. Unit ring
    b. Algebraically independent
    c. Unique factorization domain
    d. Additive identity

16. A _____ is a simple shape of Euclidean geometry consisting of those points in a plane which are at a constant distance, called the radius, from a fixed point, called the center. A _____ with center A is sometimes denoted by the symbol A.

A chord of a _____ is a line segment whose two endpoints lie on the _____.

a. Circular segment
b. Circle
c. Malfatti circles
d. Circumcircle

17. In mathematics, the term _____ has several different important meanings:

- An _____ is an equality that remains true regardless of the values of any variables that appear within it, to distinguish it from an equality which is true under more particular conditions. For this, the 'triple bar' symbol ≡ is sometimes used.
- In algebra, an _____ or _____ element of a set S with a binary operation Â· is an element e that, when combined with any element x of S, produces that same x. That is, eÂ·x = xÂ·e = x for all x in S.
    - The _____ function from a set S to itself, often denoted id or id$_S$, s the function such that i = x for all x in S. This function serves as the _____ element in the set of all functions from S to itself with respect to function composition.
    - In linear algebra, the _____ matrix of size n is the n-by-n square matrix with ones on the main diagonal and zeros elsewhere. This matrix serves as the _____ with respect to matrix multiplication.

A common example of the first meaning is the trigonometric _____

$$\sin^2 \theta + \cos^2 \theta = 1$$

which is true for all real values of θ, as opposed to

$$\cos \theta = 1,$$

which is true only for some values of θ, not all. For example, the latter equation is true when $\theta = 0$, false when $\theta = 2$

The concepts of 'additive _____' and 'multiplicative _____' are central to the Peano axioms. The number 0 is the 'additive _____' for integers, real numbers, and complex numbers. For the real numbers, for all $a \in \mathbb{R}$,

$$0 + a = a,$$

$$a + 0 = a, \text{ and}$$

$$0 + 0 = 0.$$

Similarly, The number 1 is the 'multiplicative _____' for integers, real numbers, and complex numbers.

   a. Intersection
   b. ARIA
   c. Action
   d. Identity

18. The _____ is a rule which states that when you add or multiply numbers, changing the order doesn't change the result.
   a. Conditional event algebra
   b. Semigroupoid
   c. Coimage
   d. Commutative law

19. In mathematics, _____ is a property that a binary operation can have. It means that, within an expression containing two or more of the same associative operators in a row, the order that the operations are performed does not matter as long as the sequence of the operands is not changed. That is, rearranging the parentheses in such an expression will not change its value.
   a. Associativity
   b. Unital
   c. Idempotence
   d. Algebraically closed

20. A _____ is a software program that facilitates symbolic mathematics. The core functionality of a CAS is manipulation of mathematical expressions in symbolic form.

Chapter 1. Operations on Whole Numbers 7

The symbolic manipulations supported typically include

- simplification to the smallest possible expression or some standard form, including automatic simplification with assumptions and simplification with constraints
- substitution of symbolic, functors or numeric values for expressions
- change of form of expressions: expanding products and powers, partial and full factorization, rewriting as partial fractions, constraint satisfaction, rewriting trigonometric functions as exponentials, etc.
- partial and total differentiation
- symbolic constrained and unconstrained global optimization
- solution of linear and some non-linear equations over various domains
- solution of some differential and difference equations
- taking some limits
- some indefinite and definite integration, including multidimensional integrals
- integral transforms
- arbitrary-precision numeric operations
- Series operations such as expansion, summation and products
- matrix operations including products, inverses, etc.
- display of mathematical expressions in two-dimensional mathematical form, often using typesetting systems similar to TeX
- add-ons for use in applied mathematics such as physics packages for physical computation
- plotting graphs and parametric plots of functions in two and three dimensions, and animating them
- APIs for linking it on an external program such as a database, or using in a programming language to use the _____
- drawing charts and diagrams
- string manipulation such as matching and searching
- statistical computation
- Theorem proving and verification
- graphic production and editing such as CGI and signal processing as image processing
- sound synthesis

Many also include a programming language, allowing users to implement their own algorithms.

Some _____ s focus on a specific area of application; these are typically developed in academia and are free.

a. 2-3 heap
b. 120-cell
c. 1-center problem
d. Computer algebra system

21. The _____ is the length of the line that bounds an area In the special case where the area is circular, the _____ is known as the circumference.

a. Multilateration
b. Reflection symmetry
c. Concyclic
d. Perimeter

22. In geometry, a _____ is defined as a quadrilateral where all four of its angles are right angles.
a. Cantor-Dedekind axiom
b. Point group in two dimensions
c. Polytope
d. Rectangle

23. In mathematics and in the sciences, a _____ (plural: _____e, formulæ or _____s) is a concise way of expressing information symbolically (as in a mathematical or chemical _____), or a general relationship between quantities. One of many famous _____e is Albert Einstein's $E = mc^2$ (see special relativity

In mathematics, a _____ is a key to solve an equation with variables. For example, the problem of determining the volume of a sphere is one that requires a significant amount of integral calculus to solve.

a. 120-cell
b. 1-center problem
c. 2-3 heap
d. Formula

24. _____ is a quantity expressing the two-dimensional size of a defined part of a surface, typically a region bounded by a closed curve. The term surface _____ refers to the total _____ of the exposed surface of a 3-dimensional solid, such as the sum of the _____s of the exposed sides of a polyhedron. _____ is an important invariant in the differential geometry of surfaces.
a. A Mathematical Theory of Communication
b. A chemical equation
c. A posteriori
d. Area

25. A _____ is a device for performing mathematical calculations, distinguished from a computer by having a limited problem solving ability and an interface optimized for interactive calculation rather than programming. _____s can be hardware or software, and mechanical or electronic, and are often built into devices such as PDAs or mobile phones.

Modern electronic _____s are generally small, digital, and usually inexpensive.

a. 2-3 heap
b. 120-cell
c. Calculator
d. 1-center problem

26. The traditional names for the parts of the formula c − b = a, are _____ (c) − subtrahend (b) = difference (a). The words _____ and subtrahend are uncommon in modern usage. Instead we say that c and −b are terms, and treat subtraction as addition of the opposite. The answer is still called the difference.
    a. Lowest common denominator
    b. Plus and minus signs
    c. Multiplication
    d. Minuend

27. In mathematics, the _____ of a number n is the number that, when added to n, yields zero. The _____ of n is denoted −n. For example, 7 is −7, because 7 + (−7) = 0, and the _____ of −0.3 is 0.3, because −0.3 + 0.3 = 0.
    a. Arity
    b. Associativity
    c. Algebraic structure
    d. Additive inverse

28. The quantity that is deducted from the minuend in subtraction is the _____.
    a. Lowest common denominator
    b. The number 0 is even.
    c. Trailing zeros
    d. Subtrahend

29. In abstract algebra, a field extension L /K is called _____ if every element of L is _____ over K. Field extensions which are not _____.

For example, the field extension R/Q, that is the field of real numbers as an extension of the field of rational numbers, is transcendental, while the field extensions C/R and Q

   a. Echo
   b. Identity
   c. Ideal
   d. Algebraic

30. In vascular plants, the _____ is the organ of a plant body that typically lies below the surface of the soil. This is not always the case, however, since a _____ can also be aerial (that is, growing above the ground) or aerating (that is, growing up above the ground or especially above water.) Furthermore, a stem normally occurring below ground is not exceptional either
    a. Root
    b. 2-3 heap
    c. 120-cell
    d. 1-center problem

31. _____ involves reducing the number of significant digits in a number. The result of _____ is a 'shorter' number having fewer non-zero digits yet similar in magnitude. The result is less precise but easier to use.
    a. Sudan function
    b. Shabakh
    c. Hyper operator
    d. Rounding

32. _____ is the calculated approximation of a result which is usable even if input data may be incomplete or uncertain.

In statistics, see _____ theory, estimator.

In mathematics, approximation or _____ typically means finding upper or lower bounds of a quantity that cannot readily be computed precisely and is also an educated guess.

    a. U-statistic
    b. Estimator
    c. Estimation theory
    d. Estimation

33. In mathematics, an inequality is a statement about the relative size or order of two objects. For example 14 > 10, or 14 is _____ 10. The notation a > b means that a is _____ b and 'a' would be to the right of 'b' on a number line.
    a. Greater than
    b. Cauchy-Schwarz inequality
    c. FKG inequality
    d. Minkowski inequality

34. In mathematics, an _____ is a statement about the relative size or order of two objects, or about whether they are the same or not

- The notation a < b means that a is less than b.
- The notation a > b means that a is greater than b.
- The notation a ≠ b means that a is not equal to b, but does not say that one is bigger than the other or even that they can be compared in size.

In all these cases, a is not equal to b, hence, '_____'.

These relations are known as strict _____

- The notation a ≤ b means that a is less than or equal to b;
- The notation a ≥ b means that a is greater than or equal to b;

An additional use of the notation is to show that one quantity is much greater than another, normally by several orders of magnitude.

- The notation a << b means that a is much less than b.
- The notation a >> b means that a is much greater than b.

If the sense of the _____ is the same for all values of the variables for which its members are defined, then the _____ is called an 'absolute' or 'unconditional' _____. If the sense of an _____ holds only for certain values of the variables involved, but is reversed or destroyed for other values of the variables, it is called a conditional _____.

An _____ may appear unsolvable because it only states whether a number is larger or smaller than another number; but it is possible to apply the same operations for equalities to inequalities. For example, to find x for the _____ 10x > 23 one would divide 23 by 10.

a. A Mathematical Theory of Communication
b. A chemical equation
c. Inequality
d. A posteriori

35. In mathematics, an _____ in the sense of ring theory is a subring $\mathcal{O}$ of a ring R that satisfies the conditions

1. R is a ring which is a finite-dimensional algebra over the rational number field $\mathbb{Q}$
2. $\mathcal{O}$ spans R over $\mathbb{Q}$, so that $\mathbb{Q}\mathcal{O} = R$, and
3. $\mathcal{O}$ is a lattice in R.

Chapter 1. Operations on Whole Numbers

The third condition can be stated more accurately, in terms of the extension of scalars of R to the real numbers, embedding R in a real vector space. In less formal terms, additively $\mathcal{O}$ should be a free abelian group generated by a basis for R over $\mathbb{Q}$.

The leading example is the case where R is a number field K and $\mathcal{O}$ is its ring of integers. In algebraic number theory there are examples for any K other than the rational field of proper subrings of the ring of integers that are also _____s.

a. Order
b. Annihilator
c. Algebraic
d. Efficiency

36. _____ is the mathematical operation of scaling one number by another. It is one of the four basic operations in elementary arithmetic.

_____ is defined for whole numbers in terms of repeated addition; for example, 4 multiplied by 3 can be calculated by adding 3 copies of 4 together:

$$4 + 4 + 4 = 12.$$

_____ of rational numbers and real numbers is defined by systematic generalization of this basic idea.

a. Least common multiple
b. Multiplication
c. Highest common factor
d. The number 0 is even.

37. In computational complexity theory, an algorithm is said to take _____ if the asymptotic upper bound for the time it requires is proportional to the size of the input, which is usually denoted n.

Informally spoken, the running time increases linearly with the size of the input. For example, a procedure that adds up all elements of a list requires time proportional to the length of the list.

a. Constructible function
b. Time-constructible function
c. Truth table reduction
d. Linear time

Chapter 1. Operations on Whole Numbers 13

38. In algebra and computer programming, when a number or expression is both preceded and followed by a binary operation, a rule is required for which operation should be applied first; this rule is known as an _____ . From the earliest use of mathematical notation, multiplication took precedence over addition, whichever side of a number it appeared on. Thus 3 + 4 × 5 = 5 × 4 + 3 = 23.
   a. Algebraic K-theory
   b. Identity element
   c. Order of operations
   d. Isomorphism class

39. In computer science an _____ is a data structure consisting of a group of elements that are accessed by indexing. In most programming languages each element has the same data type and the _____ occupies a contiguous area of storage.

    Most programming languages have a built-in _____ data type, although what is called an _____ in the language documentation is sometimes really an associative _____.

    a. A posteriori
    b. A chemical equation
    c. A Mathematical Theory of Communication
    d. Array

40. In mathematics, and in particular in abstract algebra, distributivity is a property of binary operations that generalises the _____ law from elementary algebra.
    a. Closure with a twist
    b. General linear group
    c. Permutation
    d. Distributive

41. In mathematics, for a sequence of numbers $a_1, a_2, a_3, \ldots$ the infinite product

$$\prod_{n=1}^{\infty} a_n = a_1\, a_2\, a_3 \cdots$$

is defined to be the limit of the _____ $a_1 a_2 \ldots a_n$ as n increases without bound. The product is said to converge when the limit exists and is not zero.

a. Semi-continuity
b. Bounded variation
c. Quasiconvex function
d. Partial products

42. Exponentiation is a mathematical operation, written a^n, involving two numbers, the base a and the _____ n. When n is a positive integer, exponentiation corresponds to repeated multiplication:

$$a^n = \underbrace{a \times \cdots \times a}_{n},$$

just as multiplication by a positive integer corresponds to repeated addition:

$$a \times n = \underbrace{a + \cdots + a}_{n}.$$

The _____ is usually shown as a superscript to the right of the base. The exponentiation a^n can be read as: a raised to the n-th power, a raised to the power [of] n or possibly a raised to the _____ [of] n, or more briefly: a to the n-th power or a to the power [of] n, or even more briefly: a to the n.

a. Exponent
b. Exponential sum
c. Exponential tree
d. Exponentiating by squaring

43. _____s are payments made by a corporation to its shareholder members. When a corporation earns a profit or surplus, that money can be put to two uses: it can either be re-invested in the business, or it can be paid to the shareholders as a _____. Many corporations retain a portion of their earnings and pay the remainder as a _____.

a. GNU Privacy Guard
b. Dividend
c. 1-center problem
d. 120-cell

44. In mathematics, a _____ of an integer n is an integer which evenly divides n without leaving a remainder.

For example, 7 is a _____ of 42 because 42/7 = 6. We also say 42 is divisible by 7 or 42 is a multiple of 7 or 7 divides 42 or 7 is a factor of 42 and we usually write 7 $\mid$ 42.

a. Divisor
b. 2-3 heap
c. 1-center problem
d. 120-cell

45. In mathematics, a _____ is the end result of a division problem. It can also be expressed as the number of times the divisor divides into the dividend.
a. Limiting
b. Notation
c. Marginal cost
d. Quotient

46. In mathematics, a division is called a _____ if the divisor is zero. Such a division can be formally expressed as $\frac{a}{0}$ where a is the dividend. Whether this expression can be assigned a well-defined value depends upon the mathematical setting.
a. 2-3 heap
b. Division by Zero
c. 1-center problem
d. 120-cell

47. In mathematics, _____ and undefined are used to explain whether or not expressions have meaningful, sensible, and unambiguous values. Not all branches of mathematics come to the same conclusion.

The following expressions are undefined in all contexts, but remarks in the analysis section may apply.

a. Plugging in
b. Toy model
c. Defined
d. LHS

48. In mathematics and computer science, _____ (also base-16, hexa or base, of 16. It uses sixteen distinct symbols, most often the symbols 0-9 to represent values zero to nine, and A, B, C, D, E, F (or a through f) to represent values ten to fifteen.

Its primary use is as a human friendly representation of binary coded values, so it is often used in digital electronics and computer engineering.

a. Radix
b. Tetradecimal
c. Factoradic
d. Hexadecimal

49. Scientific notation, also sometimes known as standard form or as _____, is a way of writing numbers that accommodates values too large or small to be conveniently written in standard decimal notation. Scientific notation has a number of useful properties and is often favored by scientists, mathematicians and engineers, who work with such numbers.

In scientific notation, numbers are written in the form:

$$a \times 10^b$$

a. A posteriori
b. Exponential notation
c. A chemical equation
d. A Mathematical Theory of Communication

Chapter 2. Multiplying and Dividing Fractions   17

1. In mathematics, a _____ of an integer n is an integer which evenly divides n without leaving a remainder.

For example, 7 is a _____ of 42 because 42/7 = 6. We also say 42 is divisible by 7 or 42 is a multiple of 7 or 7 divides 42 or 7 is a factor of 42 and we usually write 7 | 42.

   a. 120-cell
   b. 2-3 heap
   c. 1-center problem
   d. Divisor

2. In mathematics, a _____ can mean either an element of the set {1, 2, 3, ...} (i.e the positive integers) or an element of the set {0, 1, 2, 3, ...} (i.e. the non-negative integers).
   a. Whole number
   b. FISH
   c. Bounded
   d. Degrees of freedom

3. In mathematics, a _____ is a natural number which has exactly two distinct natural number divisors: 1 and itself. An infinitude of _____s exists, as demonstrated by Euclid around 300 BC. The first twenty-five _____s are:

   2, 3, 5, 7, 11, 13, 17, 19, 23, 29, 31, 37, 41, 43, 47, 53, 59, 61, 67, 71, 73, 79, 83, 89, 97.

   a. Prime number
   b. Pronic number
   c. Perrin number
   d. Highly composite number

4. In mathematics, the _____ is a simple, ancient algorithm for finding all prime numbers up to a specified integer. It works efficiently for the smaller primes . It was created by Eratosthenes, an ancient Greek mathematician.
   a. 1-center problem
   b. 120-cell
   c. 2-3 heap
   d. Sieve of Eratosthenes

5. The _____ is the largest integer that is currently known to be a prime number. Graph of number of digits in largest known prime by year, since the electronic computer. Note that the vertical scale is logarithmic.

It was proven by Euclid that there are infinitely many prime numbers; thus, there is always a prime greater than the largest known prime.

a. Prime k-tuple
b. Sierpinski number
c. Largest known Prime number
d. Ruth-Aaron pair

6. A _____ number is a positive integer which has a positive divisor other than one or itself. By definition, every integer greater than one is either a prime number or a _____ number.zero and one are considered to be neither prime nor _____. For example, the integer 14 is a _____ number because it can be factored as 2 × 7.
a. Basis
b. Key server
c. Discontinuity
d. Composite

7. A _____ is a positive integer which has a positive divisor other than one or itself. In other words, if 0 < n is an integer and there are integers 1 < a, b < n such that n = a × b then n is composite. By definition, every integer greater than one is either a prime number or a _____.
a. Ruth-Aaron pair
b. Prime Pages
c. Megaprime
d. Composite number

8. In number theory, the _____s of a positive integer are the prime numbers that divide into that integer exactly, without leaving a remainder. The process of finding these numbers is called integer factorization, or prime factorization.

For a _____ p of n, the multiplicity of p is the largest exponent a for which p^a divides n.

a. Gigantic prime
b. Cunningham chain
c. Wieferich pair
d. Prime factor

9. In set theory, a _____ is a partially ordered set such that for each t ∈ T, the set {s ∈ T : s < t} is well-ordered by the relation <. For each t ∈ T, the order type of {s ∈ T : s < t} is called the height of t. The height of T itself is the least ordinal greater than the height of each element of T.

a. Tree
b. Definable numbers
c. Set-theoretic topology
d. Transitive reduction

10. In number theory, the _____ states that every natural number greater than 1 can be written as a unique product of prime numbers. For instance,

$$6936 = 2^3 \times 3 \times 17^2,$$
$$1200 = 2^4 \times 3 \times 5^2.$$

There are no other possible factorizations of 6936 or 1200 into non-negative prime numbers. The above representation collapses repeated prime factors into powers for easier identification.

a. Cyclic number
b. Dedekind sums
c. Fundamental theorem of arithmetic
d. Feit–Thompson theorem

11. In abstract algebra, a field extension L /K is called _____ if every element of L is _____ over K. Field extensions which are not _____.

For example, the field extension R/Q, that is the field of real numbers as an extension of the field of rational numbers, is transcendental, while the field extensions C/R and Q

a. Identity
b. Echo
c. Algebraic
d. Ideal

12. In mathematics, a _____ is a statement that can be proved on the basis of explicitly stated or previously agreed assumptions.
a. Disjunction introduction
b. Logical value
c. Theorem
d. Boolean function

13. In mathematics, the _____ of a real number is its numerical value without regard to its sign. So, for example, 3 is the _____ of both 3 and −3.

The _____ of a number a is denoted by $|a|$.

Generalizations of the _____ for real numbers occur in a wide variety of mathematical settings.

a. Absolute value
b. A chemical equation
c. A Mathematical Theory of Communication
d. Area hyperbolic functions

14. In mathematics, in the realm of group theory, a group is said to be _____ if it equals its own commutator subgroup if the group has no nontrivial abelian quotients.

The smallest _____ group is the alternating group A_5. More generally, any non-abelian simple group is _____ since the commutator subgroup is a normal subgroup with abelian quotient.

a. Group of Lie type
b. Free product
c. Quaternion group
d. Perfect

15. In mathematics, a _____ is defined as a positive integer which is the sum of its proper positive divisors, that is, the sum of the positive divisors excluding the number itself. Equivalently, a _____ is a number that is half the sum of all of its positive divisors, or = 2n.

The first _____ is 6, because 1, 2, and 3 are its proper positive divisors, and 1 + 2 + 3 = 6.

a. Leonardo numbers
b. Nonhypotenuse number
c. Blum integer
d. Perfect number

16. A _____ is a software program that facilitates symbolic mathematics. The core functionality of a CAS is manipulation of mathematical expressions in symbolic form.

Chapter 2. Multiplying and Dividing Fractions

The symbolic manipulations supported typically include

- simplification to the smallest possible expression or some standard form, including automatic simplification with assumptions and simplification with constraints
- substitution of symbolic, functors or numeric values for expressions
- change of form of expressions: expanding products and powers, partial and full factorization, rewriting as partial fractions, constraint satisfaction, rewriting trigonometric functions as exponentials, etc.
- partial and total differentiation
- symbolic constrained and unconstrained global optimization
- solution of linear and some non-linear equations over various domains
- solution of some differential and difference equations
- taking some limits
- some indefinite and definite integration, including multidimensional integrals
- integral transforms
- arbitrary-precision numeric operations
- Series operations such as expansion, summation and products
- matrix operations including products, inverses, etc.
- display of mathematical expressions in two-dimensional mathematical form, often using typesetting systems similar to TeX
- add-ons for use in applied mathematics such as physics packages for physical computation
- plotting graphs and parametric plots of functions in two and three dimensions, and animating them
- APIs for linking it on an external program such as a database, or using in a programming language to use the _____
- drawing charts and diagrams
- string manipulation such as matching and searching
- statistical computation
- Theorem proving and verification
- graphic production and editing such as CGI and signal processing as image processing
- sound synthesis

Many also include a programming language, allowing users to implement their own algorithms.

Some _____s focus on a specific area of application; these are typically developed in academia and are free.

a. 2-3 heap
b. 120-cell
c. 1-center problem
d. Computer algebra system

17. A vulgar fraction (or common fraction) is a rational number written as one integer (the numerator) divided by a non-zero integer (the denominator).

A vulgar fraction is said to be a _____ if the absolute value of the numerator is less than the absolute value of the denominator--that is, if the absolute value of the entire fraction is less than 1.

a. 120-cell
b. 1-center problem
c. Proper fraction
d. Farey sequence

18. In the study of metric spaces in mathematics, there are various notions of two metrics on the same underlying space being 'the same', or _____.

In the following, M will denote a non-empty set and d_1 and d_2 will denote two metrics on M.

The two metrics d_1 and d_2 are said to be topologically _____ if they generate the same topology on M.

a. A posteriori
b. A chemical equation
c. A Mathematical Theory of Communication
d. Equivalent

19. _____ is the mathematical operation of scaling one number by another. It is one of the four basic operations in elementary arithmetic.

_____ is defined for whole numbers in terms of repeated addition; for example, 4 multiplied by 3 can be calculated by adding 3 copies of 4 together:

$$4 + 4 + 4 = 12.$$

_____ of rational numbers and real numbers is defined by systematic generalization of this basic idea.

a. Multiplication
b. Highest common factor
c. Least common multiple
d. The number 0 is even.

20. A _____ is a device for performing mathematical calculations, distinguished from a computer by having a limited problem solving ability and an interface optimized for interactive calculation rather than programming. _____s can be hardware or software, and mechanical or electronic, and are often built into devices such as PDAs or mobile phones.

Modern electronic _____s are generally small, digital, and usually inexpensive.

a. Calculator
b. 1-center problem
c. 2-3 heap
d. 120-cell

21. _____ is the calculated approximation of a result which is usable even if input data may be incomplete or uncertain.

In statistics, see _____ theory, estimator.

In mathematics, approximation or _____ typically means finding upper or lower bounds of a quantity that cannot readily be computed precisely and is also an educated guess .

a. Estimator
b. Estimation theory
c. U-statistic
d. Estimation

22. In mathematics, the multiplicative inverse of a number x, denoted 1/x or x^{-1}, is the number which, when multiplied by x, yields 1. The multiplicative inverse of x is also called the _____ of x.
a. 1-center problem
b. 2-3 heap
c. Reciprocal
d. 120-cell

23. In mathematics, a _____ is the end result of a division problem. It can also be expressed as the number of times the divisor divides into the dividend.
a. Quotient
b. Notation
c. Marginal cost
d. Limiting

Chapter 3. Adding and Subtracting Fractions

1. In mathematics the _____ of a set which is equipped with the operation of addition is an element which, when added to any element x in the set, yields x. One of the most familiar additive identities is the number 0 from elementary mathematics, but additive identities occur in other mathematical structures where addition is defined, such as in groups and rings.

  - The _____ familiar from elementary mathematics is zero, denoted 0. For example,

    5 + 0 = 5 = 0 + 5.

  - In the natural numbers N and all of its supersets, the _____ is 0. Thus for any one of these numbers n,

    n + 0 = n = 0 + n.

  Let N be a set which is closed under the operation of addition, denoted +. An _____ for N is any element e such that for any element n in N,

    e + n = n = n + e.

  a. Unique factorization domain
  b. Unit ring
  c. Algebraically independent
  d. Additive identity

2. A _____ is a software program that facilitates symbolic mathematics. The core functionality of a CAS is manipulation of mathematical expressions in symbolic form.

Chapter 3. Adding and Subtracting Fractions 25

The symbolic manipulations supported typically include

- simplification to the smallest possible expression or some standard form, including automatic simplification with assumptions and simplification with constraints
- substitution of symbolic, functors or numeric values for expressions
- change of form of expressions: expanding products and powers, partial and full factorization, rewriting as partial fractions, constraint satisfaction, rewriting trigonometric functions as exponentials, etc.
- partial and total differentiation
- symbolic constrained and unconstrained global optimization
- solution of linear and some non-linear equations over various domains
- solution of some differential and difference equations
- taking some limits
- some indefinite and definite integration, including multidimensional integrals
- integral transforms
- arbitrary-precision numeric operations
- Series operations such as expansion, summation and products
- matrix operations including products, inverses, etc.
- display of mathematical expressions in two-dimensional mathematical form, often using typesetting systems similar to TeX
- add-ons for use in applied mathematics such as physics packages for physical computation
- plotting graphs and parametric plots of functions in two and three dimensions, and animating them
- APIs for linking it on an external program such as a database, or using in a programming language to use the _____
- drawing charts and diagrams
- string manipulation such as matching and searching
- statistical computation
- Theorem proving and verification
- graphic production and editing such as CGI and signal processing as image processing
- sound synthesis

Many also include a programming language, allowing users to implement their own algorithms.

Some _____s focus on a specific area of application; these are typically developed in academia and are free.

a. 1-center problem
b. 120-cell
c. 2-3 heap
d. Computer algebra system

3. In mathematics, the _____ or least common denominator is the least common multiple of the denominators of a set of vulgar fractions. It is the smallest positive integer that is a multiple of the denominators. For instance, the _____ of

$$\left\{\frac{5}{12}, \frac{11}{18}\right\}$$

is 36 because the least common multiple of 12 and 18 is 36.

a. Highest common factor
b. The number 0 is even.
c. Lowest common denominator
d. Subtrahend

4. In mathematics, the term _____ has several different important meanings:

- An _____ is an equality that remains true regardless of the values of any variables that appear within it, to distinguish it from an equality which is true under more particular conditions. For this, the 'triple bar' symbol ≡ is sometimes used.
- In algebra, an _____ or _____ element of a set S with a binary operation Â· is an element e that, when combined with any element x of S, produces that same x. That is, eÂ·x = xÂ·e = x for all x in S.
  - The _____ function from a set S to itself, often denoted id or id$_S$, s the function such that i = x for all x in S. This function serves as the _____ element in the set of all functions from S to itself with respect to function composition.
  - In linear algebra, the _____ matrix of size n is the n-by-n square matrix with ones on the main diagonal and zeros elsewhere. This matrix serves as the _____ with respect to matrix multiplication.

A common example of the first meaning is the trigonometric _____

$$\sin^2\theta + \cos^2\theta = 1$$

which is true for all real values of θ, as opposed to

$$\cos\theta = 1,$$

which is true only for some values of θ, not all. For example, the latter equation is true when $\theta = 0$, false when $\theta = 2$

Chapter 3. Adding and Subtracting Fractions

The concepts of 'additive _____' and 'multiplicative _____' are central to the Peano axioms. The number 0 is the 'additive _____' for integers, real numbers, and complex numbers. For the real numbers, for all $a \in \mathbb{R}$,

$$0 + a = a,$$

$$a + 0 = a, \text{ and}$$

$$0 + 0 = 0.$$

Similarly, The number 1 is the 'multiplicative _____' for integers, real numbers, and complex numbers.

a. ARIA
b. Action
c. Intersection
d. Identity

5. In abstract algebra, a field extension L /K is called _____ if every element of L is _____ over K. Field extensions which are not _____.

For example, the field extension R/Q, that is the field of real numbers as an extension of the field of rational numbers, is transcendental, while the field extensions C/R and Q

a. Identity
b. Ideal
c. Algebraic
d. Echo

6. In arithmetic and number theory, the _____ or lowest common multiple or smallest common multiple of two integers a and b is the smallest positive integer that is a multiple of both a and b. Since it is a multiple, it can be divided by a and b without a remainder. If either a or b is 0, so that there is no such positive integer, then lc is defined to be zero.

a. Plus and minus signs
b. Plus-minus sign
c. Least common multiple
d. Lowest common denominator

7. The framework of quantum mechanics requires a careful definition of _____, and a thorough discussion of its practical and philosophical implications.

_____ is viewed in different ways in the many interpretations of quantum mechanics; however, despite the considerable philosophical differences, they almost universally agree on the practical question of what results from a routine quantum-physics laboratory _____. To describe this, a simple framework to use is the Copenhagen interpretation, and it will be implicitly used in this section; the utility of this approach has been verified countless times, and all other interpretations are necessarily constructed so as to give the same quantitative predictions as this in almost every case.

a. 1-center problem
b. Fundamental units
c. Dynamic range
d. Measurement

8. A _____ is a device for performing mathematical calculations, distinguished from a computer by having a limited problem solving ability and an interface optimized for interactive calculation rather than programming. _____s can be hardware or software, and mechanical or electronic, and are often built into devices such as PDAs or mobile phones.

Modern electronic _____s are generally small, digital, and usually inexpensive.

a. 120-cell
b. 2-3 heap
c. 1-center problem
d. Calculator

9. In economics, business, retail, and accounting, a _____ is the value of money that has been used up to produce something, and hence is not available for use anymore. In business, the _____ may be one of acquisition, in which case the amount of money expended to acquire it is counted as _____. In this case, money is the input that is gone in order to acquire the thing.

a. 1-center problem
b. 2-3 heap
c. 120-cell
d. Cost

Chapter 4. Decimals

1. In a positional numeral system, the decimal separator is a symbol used to mark the boundary between the integral and the fractional parts of a decimal numeral. When used in context of Arabic numerals, terms implying the symbol used are _____ and decimal comma.

   The decimal separator is mathematically a radix point.

   a. Hexadecimal
   b. Fibonacci coding
   c. Tetradecimal
   d. Decimal point

2. In mathematics, the _____ of a real number is its numerical value without regard to its sign. So, for example, 3 is the _____ of both 3 and −3.

   The _____ of a number a is denoted by $|a|$.

   Generalizations of the _____ for real numbers occur in a wide variety of mathematical settings.

   a. A Mathematical Theory of Communication
   b. Absolute value
   c. A chemical equation
   d. Area hyperbolic functions

3. _____ is a numeral system in which each position is related to the next by a constant multiplier, a common ratio, called the base or radix of that numeral system.
   a. NegaFibonacci coding
   b. Negative base
   c. Place value
   d. Cyrillic numerals

4. In vascular plants, the _____ is the organ of a plant body that typically lies below the surface of the soil. This is not always the case, however, since a _____ can also be aerial (that is, growing above the ground) or aerating (that is, growing up above the ground or especially above water.) Furthermore, a stem normally occurring below ground is not exceptional either
   a. 1-center problem
   b. 2-3 heap
   c. 120-cell
   d. Root

5. _____ involves reducing the number of significant digits in a number. The result of _____ is a 'shorter' number having fewer non-zero digits yet similar in magnitude. The result is less precise but easier to use.
   a. Sudan function
   b. Hyper operator
   c. Shabakh
   d. Rounding

6. In the study of metric spaces in mathematics, there are various notions of two metrics on the same underlying space being 'the same', or _____.

In the following, M will denote a non-empty set and d_1 and d_2 will denote two metrics on M.

The two metrics d_1 and d_2 are said to be topologically _____ if they generate the same topology on M.

   a. A posteriori
   b. A chemical equation
   c. A Mathematical Theory of Communication
   d. Equivalent

7. A _____ is a software program that facilitates symbolic mathematics. The core functionality of a CAS is manipulation of mathematical expressions in symbolic form.

The symbolic manipulations supported typically include

- simplification to the smallest possible expression or some standard form, including automatic simplification with assumptions and simplification with constraints
- substitution of symbolic, functors or numeric values for expressions
- change of form of expressions: expanding products and powers, partial and full factorization, rewriting as partial fractions, constraint satisfaction, rewriting trigonometric functions as exponentials, etc.
- partial and total differentiation
- symbolic constrained and unconstrained global optimization
- solution of linear and some non-linear equations over various domains
- solution of some differential and difference equations
- taking some limits
- some indefinite and definite integration, including multidimensional integrals
- integral transforms
- arbitrary-precision numeric operations
- Series operations such as expansion, summation and products
- matrix operations including products, inverses, etc.
- display of mathematical expressions in two-dimensional mathematical form, often using typesetting systems similar to TeX
- add-ons for use in applied mathematics such as physics packages for physical computation
- plotting graphs and parametric plots of functions in two and three dimensions, and animating them
- APIs for linking it on an external program such as a database, or using in a programming language to use the _____
- drawing charts and diagrams
- string manipulation such as matching and searching
- statistical computation
- Theorem proving and verification
- graphic production and editing such as CGI and signal processing as image processing
- sound synthesis

Many also include a programming language, allowing users to implement their own algorithms.

Some _____s focus on a specific area of application; these are typically developed in academia and are free.

a. 1-center problem
b. Computer algebra system
c. 2-3 heap
d. 120-cell

Chapter 4. Decimals

8. A _____ is a device for performing mathematical calculations, distinguished from a computer by having a limited problem solving ability and an interface optimized for interactive calculation rather than programming. _____s can be hardware or software, and mechanical or electronic, and are often built into devices such as PDAs or mobile phones.

Modern electronic _____s are generally small, digital, and usually inexpensive.

   a. 1-center problem
   b. 120-cell
   c. 2-3 heap
   d. Calculator

9. In mathematics the _____ of a set which is equipped with the operation of addition is an element which, when added to any element x in the set, yields x. One of the most familiar additive identities is the number 0 from elementary mathematics, but additive identities occur in other mathematical structures where addition is defined, such as in groups and rings.

   - The _____ familiar from elementary mathematics is zero, denoted 0. For example,

   $5 + 0 = 5 = 0 + 5$.

   - In the natural numbers N and all of its supersets, the _____ is 0. Thus for any one of these numbers n,

   $n + 0 = n = 0 + n$.

Let N be a set which is closed under the operation of addition, denoted +. An _____ for N is any element e such that for any element n in N,

   $e + n = n = n + e$.

   a. Unit ring
   b. Algebraically independent
   c. Unique factorization domain
   d. Additive identity

Chapter 4. Decimals   33

10. In mathematics, the term _____ has several different important meanings:

- An _____ is an equality that remains true regardless of the values of any variables that appear within it, to distinguish it from an equality which is true under more particular conditions. For this, the 'triple bar' symbol ≡ is sometimes used.
- In algebra, an _____ or _____ element of a set S with a binary operation Â· is an element e that, when combined with any element x of S, produces that same x. That is, eÂ·x = xÂ·e = x for all x in S.
    - The _____ function from a set S to itself, often denoted id or id$_S$, s the function such that i = x for all x in S. This function serves as the _____ element in the set of all functions from S to itself with respect to function composition.
    - In linear algebra, the _____ matrix of size n is the n-by-n square matrix with ones on the main diagonal and zeros elsewhere. This matrix serves as the _____ with respect to matrix multiplication.

A common example of the first meaning is the trigonometric _____

$$\sin^2 \theta + \cos^2 \theta = 1$$

which is true for all real values of θ, as opposed to

$$\cos \theta = 1,$$

which is true only for some values of θ, not all. For example, the latter equation is true when $\theta = 0$, false when $\theta = 2$

The concepts of 'additive _____' and 'multiplicative _____' are central to the Peano axioms. The number 0 is the 'additive _____' for integers, real numbers, and complex numbers. For the real numbers, for all $a \in \mathbb{R}$,

$$0 + a = a,$$

$$a + 0 = a, \text{and}$$

$$0 + 0 = 0.$$

Similarly, The number 1 is the 'multiplicative _____' for integers, real numbers, and complex numbers.

a. Intersection
b. Action
c. ARIA
d. Identity

Chapter 4. Decimals

11. In abstract algebra, a field extension L /K is called _____ if every element of L is _____ over K. Field extensions which are not _____.

For example, the field extension R/Q, that is the field of real numbers as an extension of the field of rational numbers, is transcendental, while the field extensions C/R and Q

   a. Ideal
   b. Algebraic
   c. Echo
   d. Identity

12. _____, also sometimes known as standard form or as exponential notation, is a way of writing numbers that accommodates values too large or small to be conveniently written in standard decimal notation. _____ has a number of useful properties and is often favored by scientists, mathematicians and engineers, who work with such numbers.

In _____, numbers are written in the form:

$$a \times 10^b$$

   a. Scientific notation
   b. 1-center problem
   c. Leading zero
   d. Radix point

13. The _____ is the distance around a closed curve. _____ is a kind of perimeter.

The _____ of a circle is the length around it.

   a. Flatness
   b. Brascamp-Lieb inequality
   c. Circumference
   d. Compactness measure of a shape

14. A _____ is a simple shape of Euclidean geometry consisting of those points in a plane which are at a constant distance, called the radius, from a fixed point, called the center. A _____ with center A is sometimes denoted by the symbol A.

A chord of a _____ is a line segment whose two endpoints lie on the _____.

a. Circular segment
b. Circle
c. Circumcircle
d. Malfatti circles

15. A _____ is one of the basic shapes of geometry: a polygon with three corners or vertices and three sides or edges which are line segments. A _____ with vertices A, B, and C is denoted ABC.

In Euclidean geometry any three non-collinear points determine a unique _____ and a unique plane.

a. Kepler triangle
b. Fuhrmann circle
c. Triangle
d. 1-center problem

16. _____ is the mathematical operation of scaling one number by another. It is one of the four basic operations in elementary arithmetic.

_____ is defined for whole numbers in terms of repeated addition; for example, 4 multiplied by 3 can be calculated by adding 3 copies of 4 together:

$$4 + 4 + 4 = 12.$$

_____ of rational numbers and real numbers is defined by systematic generalization of this basic idea.

a. Highest common factor
b. Least common multiple
c. The number 0 is even.
d. Multiplication

17. _____ is the calculated approximation of a result which is usable even if input data may be incomplete or uncertain.

In statistics, see _____ theory, estimator.

In mathematics, approximation or _____ typically means finding upper or lower bounds of a quantity that cannot readily be computed precisely and is also an educated guess .

a. U-statistic
b. Estimation theory
c. Estimation
d. Estimator

18. Exponentiation is a mathematical operation, written a^n, involving two numbers, the base a and the _____ n. When n is a positive integer, exponentiation corresponds to repeated multiplication:

$$a^n = \underbrace{a \times \cdots \times a}_{n},$$

just as multiplication by a positive integer corresponds to repeated addition:

$$a \times n = \underbrace{a + \cdots + a}_{n}.$$

The _____ is usually shown as a superscript to the right of the base. The exponentiation a^n can be read as: a raised to the n-th power, a raised to the power [of] n or possibly a raised to the _____ [of] n, or more briefly: a to the n-th power or a to the power [of] n, or even more briefly: a to the n.

a. Exponential sum
b. Exponent
c. Exponentiating by squaring
d. Exponential tree

19. In mathematics, an _____ in the sense of ring theory is a subring $\mathcal{O}$ of a ring R that satisfies the conditions

1. R is a ring which is a finite-dimensional algebra over the rational number field $\mathbb{Q}$
2. $\mathcal{O}$ spans R over $\mathbb{Q}$, so that $\mathbb{Q}\mathcal{O} = R$, and
3. $\mathcal{O}$ is a lattice in R.

The third condition can be stated more accurately, in terms of the extension of scalars of R to the real numbers, embedding R in a real vector space. In less formal terms, additively $\mathcal{O}$ should be a free abelian group generated by a basis for R over $\mathbb{Q}$.

The leading example is the case where R is a number field K and $\mathcal{O}$ is its ring of integers. In algebraic number theory there are examples for any K other than the rational field of proper subrings of the ring of integers that are also _____ s.

a. Algebraic
b. Order
c. Efficiency
d. Annihilator

20. In algebra and computer programming, when a number or expression is both preceded and followed by a binary operation, a rule is required for which operation should be applied first; this rule is known as an _____ . From the earliest use of mathematical notation, multiplication took precedence over addition, whichever side of a number it appeared on. Thus 3 + 4 × 5 = 5 × 4 + 3 = 23.

a. Order of operations
b. Identity element
c. Isomorphism class
d. Algebraic K-theory

21. In mathematics, a _____ can mean either an element of the set {1, 2, 3, ...} (i.e the positive integers) or an element of the set {0, 1, 2, 3, ...} (i.e. the non-negative integers).

a. Degrees of freedom
b. Bounded
c. Whole number
d. FISH

22. In mathematics and in the sciences, a _____ (plural: _____e, formulæ or _____s) is a concise way of expressing information symbolically (as in a mathematical or chemical _____), or a general relationship between quantities. One of many famous _____e is Albert Einstein's E = mc^2 (see special relativity

In mathematics, a _____ is a key to solve an equation with variables. For example, the problem of determining the volume of a sphere is one that requires a significant amount of integral calculus to solve.

a. Formula
b. 2-3 heap
c. 1-center problem
d. 120-cell

Chapter 5. Ratios and Proportions

1. A _____ is a software program that facilitates symbolic mathematics. The core functionality of a CAS is manipulation of mathematical expressions in symbolic form.

The symbolic manipulations supported typically include

- simplification to the smallest possible expression or some standard form, including automatic simplification with assumptions and simplification with constraints
- substitution of symbolic, functors or numeric values for expressions
- change of form of expressions: expanding products and powers, partial and full factorization, rewriting as partial fractions, constraint satisfaction, rewriting trigonometric functions as exponentials, etc.
- partial and total differentiation
- symbolic constrained and unconstrained global optimization
- solution of linear and some non-linear equations over various domains
- solution of some differential and difference equations
- taking some limits
- some indefinite and definite integration, including multidimensional integrals
- integral transforms
- arbitrary-precision numeric operations
- Series operations such as expansion, summation and products
- matrix operations including products, inverses, etc.
- display of mathematical expressions in two-dimensional mathematical form, often using typesetting systems similar to TeX
- add-ons for use in applied mathematics such as physics packages for physical computation
- plotting graphs and parametric plots of functions in two and three dimensions, and animating them
- APIs for linking it on an external program such as a database, or using in a programming language to use the _____
- drawing charts and diagrams
- string manipulation such as matching and searching
- statistical computation
- Theorem proving and verification
- graphic production and editing such as CGI and signal processing as image processing
- sound synthesis

Many also include a programming language, allowing users to implement their own algorithms.

Some _____s focus on a specific area of application; these are typically developed in academia and are free.

a. 2-3 heap
b. Computer algebra system
c. 120-cell
d. 1-center problem

Chapter 5. Ratios and Proportions

2. In mathematics, two quantities are called _____ if they vary in such a way that one of the quantities is a constant multiple of the other, or equivalently if they have a constant ratio.
   a. 2-3 heap
   b. 120-cell
   c. 1-center problem
   d. Proportional

3. In mathematics, the _____ of a real number is its numerical value without regard to its sign. So, for example, 3 is the _____ of both 3 and −3.

   The _____ of a number a is denoted by $|a|$.

   Generalizations of the _____ for real numbers occur in a wide variety of mathematical settings.

   a. Area hyperbolic functions
   b. A Mathematical Theory of Communication
   c. A chemical equation
   d. Absolute value

4. _____ is a special mathematical relationship between two quantities. Two quantities are called proportional if they vary in such a way that one of the quantities is a constant multiple of the other, or equivalently if they have a constant ratio.
   a. Depth
   b. Compression
   c. Discontinuity
   d. Proportionality

5. In the mathematical discipline of graph theory, a graph labeling is the assignment of labels, traditionally represented with integers, to the edges or vertices of a graph.

   Formally, given a graph G: = with V being the set of vertices and E being the set of edges, a vertex labeling is a function from some subset of the integers to the verticies of the graph. A graph with such function defined is called a vertex-_____.

   a. 120-cell
   b. 1-center problem
   c. Labeled graph
   d. 2-3 heap

Chapter 5. Ratios and Proportions

6. _____ is the mathematical operation of scaling one number by another. It is one of the four basic operations in elementary arithmetic.

_____ is defined for whole numbers in terms of repeated addition; for example, 4 multiplied by 3 can be calculated by adding 3 copies of 4 together:

$$4 + 4 + 4 = 12.$$

_____ of rational numbers and real numbers is defined by systematic generalization of this basic idea.

   a. Least common multiple
   b. The number 0 is even.
   c. Multiplication
   d. Highest common factor

7. In abstract algebra, a field extension L /K is called _____ if every element of L is _____ over K. Field extensions which are not _____.

For example, the field extension R/Q, that is the field of real numbers as an extension of the field of rational numbers, is transcendental, while the field extensions C/R and Q

   a. Ideal
   b. Identity
   c. Echo
   d. Algebraic

8. A _____ is a device for performing mathematical calculations, distinguished from a computer by having a limited problem solving ability and an interface optimized for interactive calculation rather than programming. _____s can be hardware or software, and mechanical or electronic, and are often built into devices such as PDAs or mobile phones.

Modern electronic _____s are generally small, digital, and usually inexpensive.

   a. 2-3 heap
   b. Calculator
   c. 120-cell
   d. 1-center problem

Chapter 6. Percents

1. A _____ is a software program that facilitates symbolic mathematics. The core functionality of a CAS is manipulation of mathematical expressions in symbolic form.

The symbolic manipulations supported typically include

- simplification to the smallest possible expression or some standard form, including automatic simplification with assumptions and simplification with constraints
- substitution of symbolic, functors or numeric values for expressions
- change of form of expressions: expanding products and powers, partial and full factorization, rewriting as partial fractions, constraint satisfaction, rewriting trigonometric functions as exponentials, etc.
- partial and total differentiation
- symbolic constrained and unconstrained global optimization
- solution of linear and some non-linear equations over various domains
- solution of some differential and difference equations
- taking some limits
- some indefinite and definite integration, including multidimensional integrals
- integral transforms
- arbitrary-precision numeric operations
- Series operations such as expansion, summation and products
- matrix operations including products, inverses, etc.
- display of mathematical expressions in two-dimensional mathematical form, often using typesetting systems similar to TeX
- add-ons for use in applied mathematics such as physics packages for physical computation
- plotting graphs and parametric plots of functions in two and three dimensions, and animating them
- APIs for linking it on an external program such as a database, or using in a programming language to use the _____
- drawing charts and diagrams
- string manipulation such as matching and searching
- statistical computation
- Theorem proving and verification
- graphic production and editing such as CGI and signal processing as image processing
- sound synthesis

Many also include a programming language, allowing users to implement their own algorithms.

Some _____s focus on a specific area of application; these are typically developed in academia and are free.

a. Computer algebra system
b. 1-center problem
c. 2-3 heap
d. 120-cell

2. In mathematics, a _____ is a way of expressing a number as a fraction of 100. It is often denoted using the percent sign, '%'. For example, 45% is equal to 45 / 100, or 0.45.

   a. Subtrahend
   b. Least common multiple
   c. Lowest common denominator
   d. Percentage

3. In mathematics and computer science, _____ (also base-16, hexa or base, of 16. It uses sixteen distinct symbols, most often the symbols 0-9 to represent values zero to nine, and A, B, C, D, E, F (or a through f) to represent values ten to fifteen.

Its primary use is as a human friendly representation of binary coded values, so it is often used in digital electronics and computer engineering.

   a. Factoradic
   b. Tetradecimal
   c. Radix
   d. Hexadecimal

4. _____ is a special mathematical relationship between two quantities. Two quantities are called proportional if they vary in such a way that one of the quantities is a constant multiple of the other, or equivalently if they have a constant ratio.

   a. Depth
   b. Compression
   c. Discontinuity
   d. Proportionality

5. _____ is the calculated approximation of a result which is usable even if input data may be incomplete or uncertain.

In statistics, see _____ theory, estimator.

In mathematics, approximation or _____ typically means finding upper or lower bounds of a quantity that cannot readily be computed precisely and is also an educated guess.

   a. Estimator
   b. U-statistic
   c. Estimation theory
   d. Estimation

Chapter 6. Percents

6. _____ is a fee, paid on borrowed capital. Assets lent include money, shares, consumer goods through hire purchase, major assets such as aircraft, and even entire factories in finance lease arrangements. The _____ is calculated upon the value of the assets in the same manner as upon money.
   a. Interest sensitivity gap
   b. Interest expense
   c. A Mathematical Theory of Communication
   d. Interest

7. In abstract algebra, a module S over a ring R is called _____ or irreducible if it is not the zero module 0 and if its only submodules are 0 and S. Understanding the _____ modules over a ring is usually helpful because these modules form the 'building blocks' of all other modules in a certain sense.

Abelian groups are the same as Z-modules.

   a. Basis
   b. Harmonic series
   c. Simple
   d. Derivation

8. _____ is the concept of adding accumulated interest back to the principal, so that interest is earned on interest from that moment on. The act of declaring interest to be principal is called compounding. A loan, for example, may have its interest compounded every month: in this case, a loan with $100 principal and 1% interest per month would have a balance of $101 at the end of the first month.
   a. Compound Interest
   b. Net interest margin
   c. Retained interest
   d. Net interest margin securities

9. In mathematics and in the sciences, a _____ (plural: _____e, formulæ or _____s) is a concise way of expressing information symbolically (as in a mathematical or chemical _____), or a general relationship between quantities. One of many famous _____e is Albert Einstein's $E = mc^2$ (see special relativity

In mathematics, a _____ is a key to solve an equation with variables. For example, the problem of determining the volume of a sphere is one that requires a significant amount of integral calculus to solve.

a. 1-center problem
b. 2-3 heap
c. 120-cell
d. Formula

10. In computational complexity theory, an algorithm is said to take _____ if the asymptotic upper bound for the time it requires is proportional to the size of the input, which is usually denoted n.

Informally spoken, the running time increases linearly with the size of the input. For example, a procedure that adds up all elements of a list requires time proportional to the length of the list.

a. Truth table reduction
b. Time-constructible function
c. Linear time
d. Constructible function

11. A _____ is a device for performing mathematical calculations, distinguished from a computer by having a limited problem solving ability and an interface optimized for interactive calculation rather than programming. _____s can be hardware or software, and mechanical or electronic, and are often built into devices such as PDAs or mobile phones.

Modern electronic _____s are generally small, digital, and usually inexpensive.

a. 2-3 heap
b. 120-cell
c. 1-center problem
d. Calculator

Chapter 7. Measurement

1. A _____ is a collection of data, usually presented in tabular form. Each column represents a particular variable. Each row corresponds to a given member of the _____ in question.
   a. 1-center problem
   b. Data set
   c. 2-3 heap
   d. 120-cell

2. In computational complexity theory, an algorithm is said to take _____ if the asymptotic upper bound for the time it requires is proportional to the size of the input, which is usually denoted n.

   Informally spoken, the running time increases linearly with the size of the input. For example, a procedure that adds up all elements of a list requires time proportional to the length of the list.

   a. Constructible function
   b. Time-constructible function
   c. Truth table reduction
   d. Linear time

3. The _____ of any solid, plasma, vacuum or theoretical object is how much three-dimensional space it occupies, often quantified numerically. One-dimensional figures and two-dimensional shapes are assigned zero _____ in the three-dimensional space. _____ is presented as ml or cm^3.

   _____s of straight-edged and circular shapes are calculated using arithmetic formulae.

   a. Stress-energy tensor
   b. Thermodynamic limit
   c. Cauchy momentum equation
   d. Volume

4. In the physical sciences, _____ is a measurement of the gravitational force acting on an object. Near the surface of the Earth, the acceleration due to gravity is approximately constant; this means that an object's _____ is roughly proportional to its mass.

   In commerce and in many other applications, _____ means the same as mass as that term is used in physics.

   a. Weight
   b. 2-3 heap
   c. 1-center problem
   d. 120-cell

46   *Chapter 7. Measurement*

5. In mathematics, especially in the area of abstract algebra known as combinatorial group theory, the _____ for a recursively presented group G is the algorithmic problem of deciding whether two words represent the same element. Although it is common to speak of the _____ for the group G strictly speaking it is a presentation of the group that does or does not have solvable _____. Given two finite presentations P and Q of a group G, P has solvable _____ if and only if Q does.
   a. Torsion
   b. Computational mathematics
   c. Prime ideal theorem
   d. Word problem

6. In mathematics, _____ and undefined are used to explain whether or not expressions have meaningful, sensible, and unambiguous values. Not all branches of mathematics come to the same conclusion.

The following expressions are undefined in all contexts, but remarks in the analysis section may apply.

   a. LHS
   b. Plugging in
   c. Defined
   d. Toy model

7. The framework of quantum mechanics requires a careful definition of _____, and a thorough discussion of its practical and philosophical implications.

_____ is viewed in different ways in the many interpretations of quantum mechanics; however, despite the considerable philosophical differences, they almost universally agree on the practical question of what results from a routine quantum-physics laboratory _____. To describe this, a simple framework to use is the Copenhagen interpretation, and it will be implicitly used in this section; the utility of this approach has been verified countless times, and all other interpretations are necessarily constructed so as to give the same quantitative predictions as this in almost every case.

   a. Fundamental units
   b. 1-center problem
   c. Dynamic range
   d. Measurement

8. In mathematics, the _____ of a real number is its numerical value without regard to its sign. So, for example, 3 is the _____ of both 3 and −3.

The _____ of a number a is denoted by $|a|$.

Generalizations of the _____ for real numbers occur in a wide variety of mathematical settings.

a. A chemical equation
b. A Mathematical Theory of Communication
c. Area hyperbolic functions
d. Absolute value

9. In mathematics the _____ of a set which is equipped with the operation of addition is an element which, when added to any element x in the set, yields x. One of the most familiar additive identities is the number 0 from elementary mathematics, but additive identities occur in other mathematical structures where addition is defined, such as in groups and rings.

- The _____ familiar from elementary mathematics is zero, denoted 0. For example,

    5 + 0 = 5 = 0 + 5.

- In the natural numbers N and all of its supersets, the _____ is 0. Thus for any one of these numbers n,

    n + 0 = n = 0 + n.

Let N be a set which is closed under the operation of addition, denoted +. An _____ for N is any element e such that for any element n in N,

    e + n = n = n + e.

a. Algebraically independent
b. Unique factorization domain
c. Unit ring
d. Additive identity

10. In mathematics, the term _____ has several different important meanings:

- An _____ is an equality that remains true regardless of the values of any variables that appear within it, to distinguish it from an equality which is true under more particular conditions. For this, the 'triple bar' symbol ≡ is sometimes used.
- In algebra, an _____ or _____ element of a set S with a binary operation Â· is an element e that, when combined with any element x of S, produces that same x. That is, eÂ·x = xÂ·e = x for all x in S.
    - The _____ function from a set S to itself, often denoted id or id$_S$, s the function such that i = x for all x in S. This function serves as the _____ element in the set of all functions from S to itself with respect to function composition.
    - In linear algebra, the _____ matrix of size n is the n-by-n square matrix with ones on the main diagonal and zeros elsewhere. This matrix serves as the _____ with respect to matrix multiplication.

A common example of the first meaning is the trigonometric _____

$$\sin^2 \theta + \cos^2 \theta = 1$$

which is true for all real values of θ, as opposed to

$$\cos \theta = 1,$$

which is true only for some values of θ, not all. For example, the latter equation is true when $\theta = 0$, false when $\theta = 2$

The concepts of 'additive _____' and 'multiplicative _____' are central to the Peano axioms. The number 0 is the 'additive _____' for integers, real numbers, and complex numbers. For the real numbers, for all $a \in \mathbb{R}$,

$$0 + a = a,$$

$$a + 0 = a,$$ and

$$0 + 0 = 0.$$

Similarly, The number 1 is the 'multiplicative _____' for integers, real numbers, and complex numbers.

a. Action
b. Intersection
c. ARIA
d. Identity

Chapter 7. Measurement

11. In abstract algebra, a field extension L /K is called _____ if every element of L is _____ over K. Field extensions which are not _____.

For example, the field extension R/Q, that is the field of real numbers as an extension of the field of rational numbers, is transcendental, while the field extensions C/R and Q

   a. Ideal
   b. Identity
   c. Echo
   d. Algebraic

12. _____ is the mathematical operation of scaling one number by another. It is one of the four basic operations in elementary arithmetic.

_____ is defined for whole numbers in terms of repeated addition; for example, 4 multiplied by 3 can be calculated by adding 3 copies of 4 together:

$$4 + 4 + 4 = 12.$$

_____ of rational numbers and real numbers is defined by systematic generalization of this basic idea.

   a. Least common multiple
   b. Highest common factor
   c. The number 0 is even.
   d. Multiplication

13. The _____ is a decimalised system of measurement. It exists in several variations, with different choices of base units, though the choice of base units does not affect its day-to-day use. Over the last two centuries, different variants have been considered the _____.
   a. George Dantzig
   b. Nonlinear system
   c. Metric system
   d. 1-center problem

Chapter 8. Geometry

1. A _____ is a simple shape of Euclidean geometry consisting of those points in a plane which are at a constant distance, called the radius, from a fixed point, called the center. A _____ with center A is sometimes denoted by the symbol A.

A chord of a _____ is a line segment whose two endpoints lie on the _____.

   a. Malfatti circles
   b. Circular segment
   c. Circumcircle
   d. Circle

2. The _____ is the distance around a closed curve. _____ is a kind of perimeter.

The _____ of a circle is the length around it.

   a. Flatness
   b. Circumference
   c. Brascamp-Lieb inequality
   d. Compactness measure of a shape

3. In mathematics and in the sciences, a _____ (plural: _____e, formulæ or _____s) is a concise way of expressing information symbolically (as in a mathematical or chemical _____), or a general relationship between quantities. One of many famous _____e is Albert Einstein's E = mc² (see special relativity

In mathematics, a _____ is a key to solve an equation with variables. For example, the problem of determining the volume of a sphere is one that requires a significant amount of integral calculus to solve.

   a. 120-cell
   b. 2-3 heap
   c. 1-center problem
   d. Formula

4. In classical geometry, a _____ of a circle or sphere is any line segment from its center to its boundary. By extension, the _____ of a circle or sphere is the length of any such segment. The _____ is half the diameter. In science and engineering the term _____ of curvature is commonly used as a synonym for _____.

   a. Non-Euclidean geometry
   b. Radius
   c. Duoprism
   d. Birational geometry

Chapter 8. Geometry 51

5. A _____ is a software program that facilitates symbolic mathematics. The core functionality of a CAS is manipulation of mathematical expressions in symbolic form.

The symbolic manipulations supported typically include

- simplification to the smallest possible expression or some standard form, including automatic simplification with assumptions and simplification with constraints
- substitution of symbolic, functors or numeric values for expressions
- change of form of expressions: expanding products and powers, partial and full factorization, rewriting as partial fractions, constraint satisfaction, rewriting trigonometric functions as exponentials, etc.
- partial and total differentiation
- symbolic constrained and unconstrained global optimization
- solution of linear and some non-linear equations over various domains
- solution of some differential and difference equations
- taking some limits
- some indefinite and definite integration, including multidimensional integrals
- integral transforms
- arbitrary-precision numeric operations
- Series operations such as expansion, summation and products
- matrix operations including products, inverses, etc.
- display of mathematical expressions in two-dimensional mathematical form, often using typesetting systems similar to TeX
- add-ons for use in applied mathematics such as physics packages for physical computation
- plotting graphs and parametric plots of functions in two and three dimensions, and animating them
- APIs for linking it on an external program such as a database, or using in a programming language to use the _____
- drawing charts and diagrams
- string manipulation such as matching and searching
- statistical computation
- Theorem proving and verification
- graphic production and editing such as CGI and signal processing as image processing
- sound synthesis

Many also include a programming language, allowing users to implement their own algorithms.

Some _____s focus on a specific area of application; these are typically developed in academia and are free.

a. 1-center problem
b. 2-3 heap
c. Computer algebra system
d. 120-cell

6. _____ is a quantity expressing the two-dimensional size of a defined part of a surface, typically a region bounded by a closed curve. The term surface _____ refers to the total _____ of the exposed surface of a 3-dimensional solid, such as the sum of the _____s of the exposed sides of a polyhedron. _____ is an important invariant in the differential geometry of surfaces.
   a. A Mathematical Theory of Communication
   b. A posteriori
   c. Area
   d. A chemical equation

7. In mathematics, the _____ of a Euclidean space is a special point, usually denoted by the letter O, used as a fixed point of reference for the geometry of the surrounding space. In a Cartesian coordinate system, the _____ is the point where the axes of the system intersect. In Euclidean geometry, the _____ may be chosen freely as any convenient point of reference.
   a. Interval
   b. OMAC
   c. Autonomous system
   d. Origin

8. In mathematics, the _____ of a real number is its numerical value without regard to its sign. So, for example, 3 is the _____ of both 3 and −3.

The _____ of a number a is denoted by $|a|$.

Generalizations of the _____ for real numbers occur in a wide variety of mathematical settings.

   a. A Mathematical Theory of Communication
   b. A chemical equation
   c. Area hyperbolic functions
   d. Absolute value

9. In geometry, a _____ is a quadrilateral with two sets of parallel sides. The opposite sides of a _____ are of equal length, and the opposite angles of a _____ are congruent. The three-dimensional counterpart of a _____ is a parallelepiped.
   a. Parallelogram
   b. 120-cell
   c. 1-center problem
   d. 2-3 heap

Chapter 8. Geometry

10. A _____ is one of the basic shapes of geometry: a polygon with three corners or vertices and three sides or edges which are line segments. A _____ with vertices A, B, and C is denoted ABC.

In Euclidean geometry any three non-collinear points determine a unique _____ and a unique plane.

 a. 1-center problem
 b. Kepler triangle
 c. Fuhrmann circle
 d. Triangle

11. In geometry, a _____ is a part of a line that is bounded by two distinct end points, and contains every point on the line between its end points. Examples of _____s include the sides of a triangle or square. More generally, when the end points are both vertices of a polygon, the _____ is either an edge if they are adjacent vertices, or otherwise a diagonal.
 a. Cuboid
 b. Golden angle
 c. Line segment
 d. Transversal line

12. In geometry and trigonometry, an _____ is the figure formed by two rays sharing a common endpoint, called the vertex of the _____. The magnitude of the _____ is the 'amount of rotation' that separates the two rays, and can be measured by considering the length of circular arc swept out when one ray is rotated about the vertex to coincide with the other. Where there is no possibility of confusion, the term '_____' is used interchangeably for both the geometric configuration itself and for its angular magnitude.
 a. A Mathematical Theory of Communication
 b. A chemical equation
 c. A posteriori
 d. Angle

13. An angle smaller than a right angle is called an _____ (less than 90 degrees).
 a. Acute angle
 b. Euclidean geometry
 c. Integral geometry
 d. Ultraparallel theorem

14. A _____ of a curve is the envelope of a family of congruent circles centered on the curve. It generalises the concept of _____ lines.

It is sometimes called the offset curve but the term 'offset' often refers also to translation.

a. Cissoid
b. Bifolium
c. Cycloid
d. Parallel

15. The existence and properties of _____ are the basis of Euclid's parallel postulate. _____ are two lines on the same plane that do not intersect even assuming that lines extend to infinity in either direction.
   a. Square wheel
   b. Vertical translation
   c. Spidron
   d. Parallel lines

16. In geometry, a _____ is a special kind of point, usually a corner of a polygon, polyhedron, or higher dimensional polytope. In the geometry of curves a _____ is a point of where the first derivative of curvature is zero. In graph theory, a _____ is the fundamental unit out of which graphs are formed
   a. Duality
   b. Dini
   c. Vertex
   d. Crib

17. In mathematics, the _____ is an approach to finding a particular solution to certain inhomogeneous ordinary differential equations and recurrence relations. It is closely related to the annihilator method, but instead of using a particular kind of differential operator in order to find the best possible form of the particular solution, a 'guess' is made as to the appropriate form, which is then tested by differentiating the resulting equation. In this sense, the _____ is less formal but more intuitive than the annihilator method.
   a. Differential algebraic equations
   b. Linear differential equation
   c. Phase line
   d. Method of undetermined coefficients

18. In geometry and trigonometry, a _____ is defined as an angle between two straight intersecting lines of ninety degrees, or one-quarter of a circle.
   a. Right angle
   b. Trigonometry
   c. Sine integral
   d. Trigonometric functions

Chapter 8. Geometry

19. An angle equal to two right angles is called a _____ (equal to 180 degrees).
    a. Householder transformation
    b. Straight angle
    c. Theorem
    d. Loomis-Whitney inequality

20. In mathematics the concept of a _____ generalizes notions such as 'length', 'area', and 'volume'. Informally, given some base set, a '_____' is any consistent assignment of 'sizes' to the subsets of the base set. Depending on the application, the 'size' of a subset may be interpreted as its physical size, the amount of something that lies within the subset, or the probability that some random process will yield a result within the subset.
    a. Congruent
    b. Lattice
    c. Cusp
    d. Measure

21. A pair of angles are complementary if the sum of their measures add up to 90 degrees.

If the two _____ are adjacent (i.e. have a common vertex and share a side, but do not have any interior points in common) their non-shared sides form a right angle.

In Euclidean geometry, the two acute angles in a right triangle are complementary, because there are 180>° in a triangle and 90>° have been accounted for by the right angle.

   a. Complementary angles
   b. Conway polyhedron notation
   c. Quincunx
   d. Hypotenuse

22. A pair of angles is _____ if their measurements add up to 180 degrees. If the two _____ angles are adjacent their non-shared sides form a straight line. The supplement of 135 would be 45.
    a. Dense
    b. Cylinder
    c. FISH
    d. Supplementary

23. A pair of angles are said to be _____ if they share the same vertex and are bounded by the same pair of lines but are opposite to each other. They are also congruent.

a. Line segment
b. Reflection symmetry
c. Hinge theorem
d. Vertical angles

24. In combinatorial mathematics, given a collection C of sets, a _____ is a set containing exactly one element from each member of the collection: it is a section of the quotient map induced by the collection. If the original sets are not disjoint, there are several different definitions. One variation is that there is a bijection f from the _____ to C such that x is an element of f
   a. Combinadic
   b. Transversal
   c. Heawood number
   d. Combinatorial design

25. In geometry, an _____ is an angle formed by two sides of a simple polygon that share an endpoint, namely, the angle on the inner side of the polygon. A simple polygon has exactly one internal angle per vertex.

If every internal angle of a polygon is at most 180 degrees, the polygon is called convex.

   a. Angle bisector
   b. Interior Angle
   c. Exterior angle
   d. Angle chasing

26. _____ are formed when a given transversal line crosses two coplanar lines. The _____ are not necessarily congruent. In the event that the _____ are congruent, these angles can be used to determine the degrees of the other angles of the parallel lines.
   a. Prismatic pentagonal tiling
   b. Corresponding angles
   c. Conformal connection
   d. Brocard circle

27. In geometry, a _____ is a polygon with six edges and six vertices. A regular _____ has Schläfli symbol {6}.

The internal angles of a regular _____ are all 120° and the _____ has 720 degrees.

a. Hexagon
b. Polygonal chain
c. Polygonal curve
d. Decagon

28. In geometry, a _____ is any five-sided polygon. A _____ may be simple or self-intersecting. The internal angles in a simple _____ total 540°.
   a. Regular octagon
   b. Triskaidecagon
   c. Star polygon
   d. Pentagon

29. An _____ is a triangle that has one internal angle larger than 90°
   a. Isotomic conjugate
   b. A chemical equation
   c. Obtuse triangle
   d. A Mathematical Theory of Communication

30. In geometry, a _____ is a polygon with four sides or edges and four vertices or corners. Sometimes, the term quadrangle is used, for etymological symmetry with triangle, and sometimes tetragon for consistency with pentagon, hexagon and so on. The interior angles of a _____ add up to 360 degrees of arc.
   a. 120-cell
   b. 2-3 heap
   c. 1-center problem
   d. Quadrilateral

31. In geometry, an _____ is a triangle in which all three sides have equal lengths. In traditional or Euclidean geometry, _____s are also equiangular; that is, all three internal angles are also equal to each other and are each 60°. They are regular polygons, and can therefore also be referred to as regular triangles.
   a. A chemical equation
   b. Equilateral triangle
   c. Isotomic conjugate
   d. A Mathematical Theory of Communication

32. In mathematics, the _____ or Pythagoras' theorem is a relation in Euclidean geometry among the three sides of a right triangle. The theorem is named after the Greek mathematician Pythagoras, who by tradition is credited with its discovery and proof, although it is often argued that knowledge of the theory predates him.. The theorem is as follows:

In any right triangle, the area of the square whose side is the hypotenuse is equal to the sum of the areas of the squares whose sides are the two legs.

    a. Pythagorean theorem
    b. 2-3 heap
    c. 1-center problem
    d. 120-cell

33. In mathematics, a _____ is a statement that can be proved on the basis of explicitly stated or previously agreed assumptions.
    a. Theorem
    b. Boolean function
    c. Disjunction introduction
    d. Logical value

34. In linear algebra, two n-by-n matrices A and B over the field K are called _____ if there exists an invertible n-by-n matrix P over K such that

$$P^{-1}AP = B.$$

One of the meanings of the term similarity transformation is such a transformation of a matrix A into a matrix B.

Similarity is an equivalence relation on the space of square matrices.

_____ matrices share many properties:

- rank
- determinant
- trace
- eigenvalues
- characteristic polynomial
- minimal polynomial
- elementary divisors

Chapter 8. Geometry

There are two reasons for these facts:

- two _____ matrices can be thought of as describing the same linear map, but with respect to different bases
- the map $X \mapsto P^{-1}XP$ is an automorphism of the associative algebra of all n-by-n matrices, as the one-object case of the above category of all matrices.

Because of this, for a given matrix A, one is interested in finding a simple 'normal form' B which is _____ to A -- the study of A then reduces to the study of the simpler matrix B.

a. Similar
b. Dense
c. Coherence
d. Blinding

35. In mathematics, an algebraic group G contains a unique maximal normal solvable subgroup; and this subgroup is closed. Its identity component is called the _____ of G.
a. Composite
b. Barycentric coordinates
c. Block size
d. Radical

36. In mathematics, a _____ of a number x is a number r such that r^2 = x, or, in other words, a number r whose square is x. Every non-negative real number x has a unique non-negative _____, called the principal _____, which is denoted with a radical symbol as $\sqrt{x}$, or, using exponent notation, as $x^{1/2}$. For example, the principal _____ of 9 is 3, denoted $\sqrt{9}$ = 3, because 3^2 = 3 × 3 = 9.
a. Square root
b. Double exponential
c. Hyperbolic functions
d. Multiplicative inverse

37. In vascular plants, the _____ is the organ of a plant body that typically lies below the surface of the soil. This is not always the case, however, since a _____ can also be aerial (that is, growing above the ground) or aerating (that is, growing up above the ground or especially above water.) Furthermore, a stem normally occurring below ground is not exceptional either

a. 2-3 heap
b. 1-center problem
c. 120-cell
d. Root

38. A _____ is the longest side of a right triangle, the side opposite of the right angle. The length of the _____ of a right triangle can be found using the Pythagorean theorem, which states that the square of the length of the _____ equals the sum of the squares of the lengths of the two other sides.

For example, if one of the other sides has a length of 3 meters and the other has a length of 4 m.

a. Hypotenuse
b. Golden angle
c. Reflection symmetry
d. Concyclic points

39. In mathematics, in the realm of group theory, a group is said to be _____ if it equals its own commutator subgroup if the group has no nontrivial abelian quotients.

The smallest _____ group is the alternating group A_5. More generally, any non-abelian simple group is _____ since the commutator subgroup is a normal subgroup with abelian quotient.

a. Free product
b. Quaternion group
c. Perfect
d. Group of Lie type

40. _____ is a part of mathematics concerned with questions of size, shape, and relative position of figures and with properties of space. _____ is one of the oldest sciences. Initially a body of practical knowledge concerning lengths, areas, and volumes, in the third century BC _____ was put into an axiomatic form by Euclid, whose treatment--Euclidean _____--set a standard for many centuries to follow.

a. 120-cell
b. 2-3 heap
c. 1-center problem
d. Geometry

41. A _____ is a device for performing mathematical calculations, distinguished from a computer by having a limited problem solving ability and an interface optimized for interactive calculation rather than programming. _____s can be hardware or software, and mechanical or electronic, and are often built into devices such as PDAs or mobile phones.

Modern electronic _____s are generally small, digital, and usually inexpensive.

   a. 120-cell
   b. Calculator
   c. 1-center problem
   d. 2-3 heap

Chapter 9. Data Analysis and Statistics

1. A _____ is a software program that facilitates symbolic mathematics. The core functionality of a CAS is manipulation of mathematical expressions in symbolic form.

The symbolic manipulations supported typically include

- simplification to the smallest possible expression or some standard form, including automatic simplification with assumptions and simplification with constraints
- substitution of symbolic, functors or numeric values for expressions
- change of form of expressions: expanding products and powers, partial and full factorization, rewriting as partial fractions, constraint satisfaction, rewriting trigonometric functions as exponentials, etc.
- partial and total differentiation
- symbolic constrained and unconstrained global optimization
- solution of linear and some non-linear equations over various domains
- solution of some differential and difference equations
- taking some limits
- some indefinite and definite integration, including multidimensional integrals
- integral transforms
- arbitrary-precision numeric operations
- Series operations such as expansion, summation and products
- matrix operations including products, inverses, etc.
- display of mathematical expressions in two-dimensional mathematical form, often using typesetting systems similar to TeX
- add-ons for use in applied mathematics such as physics packages for physical computation
- plotting graphs and parametric plots of functions in two and three dimensions, and animating them
- APIs for linking it on an external program such as a database, or using in a programming language to use the _____
- drawing charts and diagrams
- string manipulation such as matching and searching
- statistical computation
- Theorem proving and verification
- graphic production and editing such as CGI and signal processing as image processing
- sound synthesis

Many also include a programming language, allowing users to implement their own algorithms.

Some _____s focus on a specific area of application; these are typically developed in academia and are free.

   a. 120-cell
   b. 1-center problem
   c. 2-3 heap
   d. Computer algebra system

Chapter 9. Data Analysis and Statistics

2. In mathematics, an _____, or central tendency of a data set refers to a measure of the 'middle' or 'expected' value of the data set. There are many different descriptive statistics that can be chosen as a measurement of the central tendency of the data items.

An _____ is a single value that is meant to typify a list of values.

   a. A chemical equation
   b. A Mathematical Theory of Communication
   c. A posteriori
   d. Average

3. In statistics, _____ has two related meanings:

   • the arithmetic _____.
   • the expected value of a random variable, which is also called the population _____.

It is sometimes stated that the '_____' _____s average. This is incorrect if '_____' is taken in the specific sense of 'arithmetic _____' as there are different types of averages: the _____, median, and mode. For instance, average house prices almost always use the median value for the average.

For a real-valued random variable X, the _____ is the expectation of X.

   a. Mean
   b. Statistical population
   c. Probability
   d. Proportional hazards model

4. In geometry, a _____ of a triangle is a line segment joining a vertex to the midpoint of the opposing side. Every triangle has exactly three _____s; one running from each vertex to the opposite side.

The three _____s are concurrent at a point known as the triangle's centroid, or center of mass of the triangle.

   a. Correlation
   b. Percentile rank
   c. Statistical significance
   d. Median

Chapter 9. Data Analysis and Statistics

5. In statistics, the _____ is the value that occurs the most frequently in a data set or a probability distribution. In some fields, notably education, sample data are often called scores, and the sample _____ is known as the modal score.

Like the statistical mean and the median, the _____ is a way of capturing important information about a random variable or a population in a single quantity.

   a. Deltoid
   b. Function
   c. Mode
   d. Field

6. A _____ is a device for performing mathematical calculations, distinguished from a computer by having a limited problem solving ability and an interface optimized for interactive calculation rather than programming. _____s can be hardware or software, and mechanical or electronic, and are often built into devices such as PDAs or mobile phones.

Modern electronic _____s are generally small, digital, and usually inexpensive.

   a. 120-cell
   b. 1-center problem
   c. 2-3 heap
   d. Calculator

7. In signal processing, _____ is the reduction of a continuous signal to a discrete signal. A common example is the conversion of a sound wave to a sequence of samples.

A sample refers to a value or set of values at a point in time and/or space.

   a. Converse logic
   b. Decidable
   c. Sampling
   d. Disk

8. _____ or pictograph is a symbol representing a concept, object, activity, place or event by illustration. Pictography is a form of writing in which ideas are transmitted through drawing. It is a basis of cuneiform and, to some extent, hieroglyphic writing, which uses drawings also as phonetic letters or determinative rhymes.

a. Sparkline
b. Pictographs
c. Treemapping
d. Pictogram

9. In a graph theory, the _____ L

One of the earliest and most important theorems about _____s is due to Hassler Whitney, who proved that with one exceptional case the structure of G can be recovered completely from its _____.

a. Line Graph
b. Bivariegated graph
c. Vertex-transitive graph
d. Sparse graph

10. _____ are symbols representing a concept, object, activity, place or event by illustration.
a. Treemapping
b. Pictogram
c. Sparkline
d. Pictographs

11. A bar chart or _____ is a chart with rectangular bars with lengths proportional to the values that they represent. Bar charts are used for comparing two or more values. The bars can be horizontally or vertically oriented.
a. 1-center problem
b. 120-cell
c. Bar graph
d. 2-3 heap

12. A _____ is a circular chart divided into sectors, illustrating relative magnitudes or frequences or percents. In a _____, the arc length of each sector, is proportional to the quantity it represents. Together, the sectors create a full disk.
a. 2-3 heap
b. 120-cell
c. Pie chart
d. 1-center problem

13. In descriptive statistics, a _____ is a convenient way of graphically depicting the five-number summary, which consists of the smallest observation, lower quartile (Q1), median, upper quartile (Q3), and largest observation; in addition, the _____ indicates which observations, if any, are considered unusual, or outliers.
   a. Mathematical model
   b. Point-slope form
   c. Non-linear least squares
   d. Box plot

14. _____ is a process of conveying information about characters in fiction or conversation. Characters are usually present by description and through their actions, speech, and thoughts.

At performance an actor has less time to characterize and so can risk the character coming across as underdeveloped.

   a. 120-cell
   b. 1-center problem
   c. 2-3 heap
   d. Characterization

15. A _____ is is a graphical technique for presenting a data set drawn by hand or produced by a mechanical or electronic plotter. It is a graph depicting the relationship between two or more variables used, for instance, in visualising scientific data.

_____s play an important role in statistics and data analysis.

   a. Plot
   b. Lattice
   c. Dini
   d. C-35

16. In descriptive statistics, a _____ is any of the three values which divide the sorted data set into four equal parts, so that each part represents one fourth of the sampled population.

   - first _____ = lower _____ = cuts off lowest 25% of data = 25th percentile
   - second _____ = median = cuts data set in half = 50th percentile
   - third _____ = upper _____ = cuts off highest 25% of data, or lowest 75% = 75th percentile

The difference between the upper and lower _____s is called the interquartile range.

There is no universal agreement on choosing the _____ values.

Chapter 9. Data Analysis and Statistics

The formula for the position of the observation at a given percentile, y, with n data points sorted in ascending order is:

$$L_y = (n+1)(\frac{y}{100})$$

Example 4.
a. Trimean
b. Mean reciprocal rank
c. Seven-number summary
d. Quartile

17. In descriptive statistics, the _____ of a data set consists of:

1. the minimum
2. the lower quartile or first quartile
3. the median
4. the upper quartile or third quartile
5. the maximum

The _____ is sometimes represented as in the following table:

The _____ can be represented graphically using a boxplot.

- Quartile
- Order statistic
- Seven-number summary

a. Discrepancy function
b. Bayesian average
c. Computational formula for the variance
d. Five-number summary

18. In descriptive statistics, the _____ is the length of the smallest interval which contains all the data. It is calculated by subtracting the smallest observations from the greatest and provides an indication of statistical dispersion.

It is measured in the same units as the data.

a. Range
b. Class
c. Kernel
d. Bandwidth

19. In descriptive statistics, the _____ middle fifty and middle of the #s, is a measure of statistical dispersion, being equal to the difference between the third and first quartiles.

Unlike the range, the _____ is a robust statistic, having a breakdown point of 25%, and is thus often preferred to the total range.

The IQR is used to build box plots, simple graphical representations of a probability distribution.

a. Interquartile range
b. Unitized risk
c. A Mathematical Theory of Communication
d. A chemical equation

20. In statistics, an _____ is an observation that is numerically distant from the rest of the data. Statistics derived from data sets that include _____s may be misleading. For example, if one is calculating the average temperature of 10 objects in a room, and most are between 20 and 25 degrees Celsius, but an oven is at 175 °C, the median of the data may be 23 °C but the mean temperature will be between 35.5 and 40 °C.
a. A posteriori
b. A chemical equation
c. A Mathematical Theory of Communication
d. Outlier

Chapter 10. The Real Number System

1. In mathematics, a _____ can mean either an element of the set {1, 2, 3, ...} or an element of the set {0, 1, 2, 3, ...}. The latter is especially preferred in mathematical logic, set theory, and computer science.

_____s have two main purposes: they can be used for counting, and they can be used for ordering.

   a. Strong partition cardinal
   b. Cardinal numbers
   c. Natural number
   d. Suslin cardinal

2. The _____ are the set of numbers consisting of the natural numbers including 0 and their negatives. They are numbers that can be written without a fractional or decimal component, and fall within the set {... −2, −1, 0, 1, 2, ...}.
   a. A posteriori
   b. Integers
   c. A Mathematical Theory of Communication
   d. A chemical equation

3. In mathematics, a _____ is a picture of a straight line in which the integers are shown as specially-marked points evenly spaced on the line. Although this image only shows the integers from -9 to 9, the line includes all real numbers, continuing 'forever' in each direction. It is often used as an aid in teaching simple addition and subtraction, especially involving negative numbers.
   a. Point plotting
   b. Real number
   c. Number system
   d. Number line

4. In mathematics, the _____ of a Euclidean space is a special point, usually denoted by the letter O, used as a fixed point of reference for the geometry of the surrounding space. In a Cartesian coordinate system, the _____ is the point where the axes of the system intersect. In Euclidean geometry, the _____ may be chosen freely as any convenient point of reference.
   a. OMAC
   b. Interval
   c. Origin
   d. Autonomous system

5. In mathematics, a _____ can mean either an element of the set {1, 2, 3, ...} (i.e the positive integers) or an element of the set {0, 1, 2, 3, ...} (i.e. the non-negative integers).

a. FISH
b. Degrees of freedom
c. Bounded
d. Whole number

6. In mathematics, the _____ of a real number is its numerical value without regard to its sign. So, for example, 3 is the _____ of both 3 and −3.

The _____ of a number a is denoted by | a |.

Generalizations of the _____ for real numbers occur in a wide variety of mathematical settings.

a. Area hyperbolic functions
b. A Mathematical Theory of Communication
c. A chemical equation
d. Absolute value

7. A _____ is a simple shape of Euclidean geometry consisting of those points in a plane which are at a constant distance, called the radius, from a fixed point, called the center. A _____ with center A is sometimes denoted by the symbol A.

A chord of a _____ is a line segment whose two endpoints lie on the _____.

a. Malfatti circles
b. Circular segment
c. Circumcircle
d. Circle

8. A _____ number is a positive integer which has a positive divisor other than one or itself. By definition, every integer greater than one is either a prime number or a _____ number.zero and one are considered to be neither prime nor _____. For example, the integer 14 is a _____ number because it can be factored as 2 × 7.

a. Key server
b. Composite
c. Discontinuity
d. Basis

Chapter 10. The Real Number System

9. A _____ is a positive integer which has a positive divisor other than one or itself. In other words, if 0 < n is an integer and there are integers 1 < a, b < n such that n = a × b then n is composite. By definition, every integer greater than one is either a prime number or a _____.
   a. Prime Pages
   b. Ruth-Aaron pair
   c. Composite Number
   d. Megaprime

10. In mathematics, the _____s may be described informally in several different ways. The _____s include both rational numbers, such as 42 and −23/129, and irrational numbers, such as pi and the square root of two; or, a _____ can be given by an infinite decimal representation, such as 2.4871773339...., where the digits continue in some way; or, the _____s may be thought of as points on an infinitely long number line.

These descriptions of the _____s, while intuitively accessible, are not sufficiently rigorous for the purposes of pure mathematics.

   a. Pre-algebra
   b. Minkowski distance
   c. Tally marks
   d. Real number

11. In mathematics, an _____ in the sense of ring theory is a subring $\mathcal{O}$ of a ring R that satisfies the conditions

   1. R is a ring which is a finite-dimensional algebra over the rational number field $\mathbb{Q}$
   2. $\mathcal{O}$ spans R over $\mathbb{Q}$, so that $\mathbb{Q}\mathcal{O} = R$, and
   3. $\mathcal{O}$ is a lattice in R.

The third condition can be stated more accurately, in terms of the extension of scalars of R to the real numbers, embedding R in a real vector space. In less formal terms, additively $\mathcal{O}$ should be a free abelian group generated by a basis for R over $\mathbb{Q}$.

The leading example is the case where R is a number field K and $\mathcal{O}$ is its ring of integers. In algebraic number theory there are examples for any K other than the rational field of proper subrings of the ring of integers that are also _____s.

   a. Annihilator
   b. Order
   c. Efficiency
   d. Algebraic

Chapter 10. The Real Number System

12. A _____ is a software program that facilitates symbolic mathematics. The core functionality of a CAS is manipulation of mathematical expressions in symbolic form.

The symbolic manipulations supported typically include

- simplification to the smallest possible expression or some standard form, including automatic simplification with assumptions and simplification with constraints
- substitution of symbolic, functors or numeric values for expressions
- change of form of expressions: expanding products and powers, partial and full factorization, rewriting as partial fractions, constraint satisfaction, rewriting trigonometric functions as exponentials, etc.
- partial and total differentiation
- symbolic constrained and unconstrained global optimization
- solution of linear and some non-linear equations over various domains
- solution of some differential and difference equations
- taking some limits
- some indefinite and definite integration, including multidimensional integrals
- integral transforms
- arbitrary-precision numeric operations
- Series operations such as expansion, summation and products
- matrix operations including products, inverses, etc.
- display of mathematical expressions in two-dimensional mathematical form, often using typesetting systems similar to TeX
- add-ons for use in applied mathematics such as physics packages for physical computation
- plotting graphs and parametric plots of functions in two and three dimensions, and animating them
- APIs for linking it on an external program such as a database, or using in a programming language to use the _____
- drawing charts and diagrams
- string manipulation such as matching and searching
- statistical computation
- Theorem proving and verification
- graphic production and editing such as CGI and signal processing as image processing
- sound synthesis

Many also include a programming language, allowing users to implement their own algorithms.

Some _____s focus on a specific area of application; these are typically developed in academia and are free.

a. 120-cell
b. 2-3 heap
c. 1-center problem
d. Computer algebra system

Chapter 10. The Real Number System

13. In descriptive statistics, a _____ is a convenient way of graphically depicting the five-number summary, which consists of the smallest observation, lower quartile (Q1), median, upper quartile (Q3), and largest observation; in addition, the _____ indicates which observations, if any, are considered unusual, or outliers.

   a. Non-linear least squares
   b. Point-slope form
   c. Mathematical model
   d. Box plot

14. _____ is a process of conveying information about characters in fiction or conversation. Characters are usually present by description and through their actions, speech, and thoughts.

At performance an actor has less time to characterize and so can risk the character coming across as underdeveloped.

   a. 1-center problem
   b. 120-cell
   c. 2-3 heap
   d. Characterization

15. A _____ is is a graphical technique for presenting a data set drawn by hand or produced by a mechanical or electronic plotter. It is a graph depicting the relationship between two or more variables used, for instance, in visualising scientific data.

_____s play an important role in statistics and data analysis.

   a. Lattice
   b. Dini
   c. C-35
   d. Plot

16. In abstract algebra, a field extension L /K is called _____ if every element of L is _____ over K. Field extensions which are not _____.

For example, the field extension R/Q, that is the field of real numbers as an extension of the field of rational numbers, is transcendental, while the field extensions C/R and Q

a. Identity
b. Echo
c. Algebraic
d. Ideal

17. In mathematics the _____ of a set which is equipped with the operation of addition is an element which, when added to any element x in the set, yields x. One of the most familiar additive identities is the number 0 from elementary mathematics, but additive identities occur in other mathematical structures where addition is defined, such as in groups and rings.

- The _____ familiar from elementary mathematics is zero, denoted 0. For example,

5 + 0 = 5 = 0 + 5.

- In the natural numbers N and all of its supersets, the _____ is 0. Thus for any one of these numbers n,

n + 0 = n = 0 + n.

Let N be a set which is closed under the operation of addition, denoted +. An _____ for N is any element e such that for any element n in N,

e + n = n = n + e.

a. Additive identity
b. Unit ring
c. Algebraically independent
d. Unique factorization domain

18. In mathematics, the term _____ has several different important meanings:

- An _____ is an equality that remains true regardless of the values of any variables that appear within it, to distinguish it from an equality which is true under more particular conditions. For this, the 'triple bar' symbol ≡ is sometimes used.
- In algebra, an _____ or _____ element of a set S with a binary operation Â· is an element e that, when combined with any element x of S, produces that same x. That is, eÂ·x = xÂ·e = x for all x in S.
    - The _____ function from a set S to itself, often denoted id or id_S, s the function such that i = x for all x in S. This function serves as the _____ element in the set of all functions from S to itself with respect to function composition.
    - In linear algebra, the _____ matrix of size n is the n-by-n square matrix with ones on the main diagonal and zeros elsewhere. This matrix serves as the _____ with respect to matrix multiplication.

A common example of the first meaning is the trigonometric _____

$$\sin^2 \theta + \cos^2 \theta = 1$$

which is true for all real values of θ, as opposed to

$$\cos \theta = 1,$$

which is true only for some values of θ, not all. For example, the latter equation is true when $\theta = 0$, false when $\theta = 2$

The concepts of 'additive _____' and 'multiplicative _____' are central to the Peano axioms. The number 0 is the 'additive _____' for integers, real numbers, and complex numbers. For the real numbers, for all $a \in \mathbb{R}$,

$$0 + a = a,$$

$$a + 0 = a, \text{ and}$$

$$0 + 0 = 0.$$

Similarly, The number 1 is the 'multiplicative _____' for integers, real numbers, and complex numbers.

a. Action
b. ARIA
c. Intersection
d. Identity

19. In mathematics, the _____ of a number n is the number that, when added to n, yields zero. The _____ of n is denoted −n. For example, 7 is −7, because 7 + (−7) = 0, and the _____ of −0.3 is 0.3, because −0.3 + 0.3 = 0.
a. Associativity
b. Arity
c. Algebraic structure
d. Additive inverse

20. A _____ is a device for performing mathematical calculations, distinguished from a computer by having a limited problem solving ability and an interface optimized for interactive calculation rather than programming. _____s can be hardware or software, and mechanical or electronic, and are often built into devices such as PDAs or mobile phones.

Chapter 10. The Real Number System

Modern electronic _____s are generally small, digital, and usually inexpensive.

a. Calculator
b. 1-center problem
c. 2-3 heap
d. 120-cell

21. _____ is the mathematical operation of scaling one number by another. It is one of the four basic operations in elementary arithmetic.

_____ is defined for whole numbers in terms of repeated addition; for example, 4 multiplied by 3 can be calculated by adding 3 copies of 4 together:

$$4 + 4 + 4 = 12.$$

_____ of rational numbers and real numbers is defined by systematic generalization of this basic idea.

a. Least common multiple
b. Multiplication
c. Highest common factor
d. The number 0 is even.

22. In algebra and computer programming, when a number or expression is both preceded and followed by a binary operation, a rule is required for which operation should be applied first; this rule is known as an _____ . From the earliest use of mathematical notation, multiplication took precedence over addition, whichever side of a number it appeared on. Thus 3 + 4 × 5 = 5 × 4 + 3 = 23.

a. Identity element
b. Algebraic K-theory
c. Order of operations
d. Isomorphism class

23. In mathematics, _____ is a property that a binary operation can have. It means that, within an expression containing two or more of the same associative operators in a row, the order that the operations are performed does not matter as long as the sequence of the operands is not changed. That is, rearranging the parentheses in such an expression will not change its value.

Chapter 10. The Real Number System

a. Algebraically closed
b. Unital
c. Associativity
d. Idempotence

24. The _____ is a rule which states that when you add or multiply numbers, changing the order doesn't change the result.
    a. Coimage
    b. Semigroupoid
    c. Conditional event algebra
    d. Commutative law

25. In mathematics, a _____ for a number x, denoted by $1/x$ or x^{-1}, is a number which when multiplied by x yields the multiplicative identity, 1. The _____ of x is also called the reciprocal of x. The _____ of a fraction p/q is q/p.
    a. Double exponential
    b. Hyperbolic function
    c. Golden function
    d. Multiplicative inverse

26. In mathematics, the multiplicative inverse of a number x, denoted $1/x$ or x^{-1}, is the number which, when multiplied by x, yields 1. The multiplicative inverse of x is also called the _____ of x.
    a. Reciprocal
    b. 1-center problem
    c. 2-3 heap
    d. 120-cell

27. In mathematics, a division is called a _____ if the divisor is zero. Such a division can be formally expressed as $\frac{a}{0}$ where a is the dividend. Whether this expression can be assigned a well-defined value depends upon the mathematical setting.
    a. 2-3 heap
    b. Division by Zero
    c. 1-center problem
    d. 120-cell

28. In mathematics, more precisely in algebra, an _____ is a quantity that is not known, and cannot be solved for. An _____ is different from a variable, which is solvable, at least conditionally, from a given equation or set of equations. To make this distinction in an example, compare these two situations.
   a. Algebraic solution
   b. Indeterminate
   c. Immanant of a matrix
   d. Algebraic function

29. In calculus and other branches of mathematical analysis, an _____ is an algebraic expression obtained in the context of limits. Limits involving algebraic operations are often performed by replacing subexpressions by their limits; if the expression obtained after this substitution does not give enough information to determine the original limit, it is known as an _____. The _____s include 0^0, $0/0$, 1^∞, $\infty - \infty$, ∞/∞, $0\times\infty$, and ∞^0.
   a. Uniformly absolutely continuous
   b. Improper integral
   c. Exponential function can be characterized
   d. Indeterminate form

30. Exponentiation is a mathematical operation, written a^n, involving two numbers, the base a and the _____ n. When n is a positive integer, exponentiation corresponds to repeated multiplication:

$$a^n = \underbrace{a \times \cdots \times a}_{n},$$

just as multiplication by a positive integer corresponds to repeated addition:

$$a \times n = \underbrace{a + \cdots + a}_{n}.$$

The _____ is usually shown as a superscript to the right of the base. The exponentiation a^n can be read as: a raised to the n-th power, a raised to the power [of] n or possibly a raised to the _____ [of] n, or more briefly: a to the n-th power or a to the power [of] n, or even more briefly: a to the n.

   a. Exponentiating by squaring
   b. Exponential tree
   c. Exponential sum
   d. Exponent

Chapter 11. An Introduction to Algebra

1. In abstract algebra, a field extension L /K is called _____ if every element of L is _____ over K. Field extensions which are not _____.

For example, the field extension R/Q, that is the field of real numbers as an extension of the field of rational numbers, is transcendental, while the field extensions C/R and Q

   a. Identity
   b. Echo
   c. Ideal
   d. Algebraic

2. In mathematics, an _____ over a given field is an equation of the form

   P = Q

where P and Q are polynomials over that field. For example

$$y^4 + \frac{xy}{2} = \frac{x^3}{3} - xy^2 + y^2 - \frac{1}{7}$$

is an _____ over the rationals.

Note that an _____ over the rationals can always be converted to an equivalent one in which the coefficients are integers.

   a. Irreducible
   b. Euler-Worpitzky-Chen polynomials
   c. Ehrhart polynomial
   d. Algebraic equation

3. A _____ is a software program that facilitates symbolic mathematics. The core functionality of a CAS is manipulation of mathematical expressions in symbolic form.

Chapter 11. An Introduction to Algebra

The symbolic manipulations supported typically include

- simplification to the smallest possible expression or some standard form, including automatic simplification with assumptions and simplification with constraints
- substitution of symbolic, functors or numeric values for expressions
- change of form of expressions: expanding products and powers, partial and full factorization, rewriting as partial fractions, constraint satisfaction, rewriting trigonometric functions as exponentials, etc.
- partial and total differentiation
- symbolic constrained and unconstrained global optimization
- solution of linear and some non-linear equations over various domains
- solution of some differential and difference equations
- taking some limits
- some indefinite and definite integration, including multidimensional integrals
- integral transforms
- arbitrary-precision numeric operations
- Series operations such as expansion, summation and products
- matrix operations including products, inverses, etc.
- display of mathematical expressions in two-dimensional mathematical form, often using typesetting systems similar to TeX
- add-ons for use in applied mathematics such as physics packages for physical computation
- plotting graphs and parametric plots of functions in two and three dimensions, and animating them
- APIs for linking it on an external program such as a database, or using in a programming language to use the _____
- drawing charts and diagrams
- string manipulation such as matching and searching
- statistical computation
- Theorem proving and verification
- graphic production and editing such as CGI and signal processing as image processing
- sound synthesis

Many also include a programming language, allowing users to implement their own algorithms.

Some _____s focus on a specific area of application; these are typically developed in academia and are free.

a. 1-center problem
b. Computer algebra system
c. 2-3 heap
d. 120-cell

4. _____ is the mathematical operation of scaling one number by another. It is one of the four basic operations in elementary arithmetic.

_____ is defined for whole numbers in terms of repeated addition; for example, 4 multiplied by 3 can be calculated by adding 3 copies of 4 together:

$$4 + 4 + 4 = 12.$$

_____ of rational numbers and real numbers is defined by systematic generalization of this basic idea.

a. Multiplication
b. Least common multiple
c. Highest common factor
d. The number 0 is even.

5. In mathematics, the _____ of a real number is its numerical value without regard to its sign. So, for example, 3 is the _____ of both 3 and −3.

The _____ of a number a is denoted by $|a|$.

Generalizations of the _____ for real numbers occur in a wide variety of mathematical settings.

a. Absolute value
b. A chemical equation
c. A Mathematical Theory of Communication
d. Area hyperbolic functions

6. In mathematics, an _____ in the sense of ring theory is a subring $\mathcal{O}$ of a ring R that satisfies the conditions

1. R is a ring which is a finite-dimensional algebra over the rational number field $\mathbb{Q}$
2. $\mathcal{O}$ spans R over $\mathbb{Q}$, so that $\mathbb{Q}\mathcal{O} = R$, and
3. $\mathcal{O}$ is a lattice in R.

The third condition can be stated more accurately, in terms of the extension of scalars of R to the real numbers, embedding R in a real vector space. In less formal terms, additively $\mathcal{O}$ should be a free abelian group generated by a basis for R over $\mathbb{Q}$.

The leading example is the case where R is a number field K and $\mathcal{O}$ is its ring of integers. In algebraic number theory there are examples for any K other than the rational field of proper subrings of the ring of integers that are also _____s.

a. Order
b. Annihilator
c. Algebraic
d. Efficiency

7. In algebra and computer programming, when a number or expression is both preceded and followed by a binary operation, a rule is required for which operation should be applied first; this rule is known as an _____ . From the earliest use of mathematical notation, multiplication took precedence over addition, whichever side of a number it appeared on. Thus 3 + 4 × 5 = 5 × 4 + 3 = 23.
    a. Identity element
    b. Algebraic K-theory
    c. Order of operations
    d. Isomorphism class

8. A _____ is a device for performing mathematical calculations, distinguished from a computer by having a limited problem solving ability and an interface optimized for interactive calculation rather than programming. _____s can be hardware or software, and mechanical or electronic, and are often built into devices such as PDAs or mobile phones.

Modern electronic _____s are generally small, digital, and usually inexpensive.

    a. Calculator
    b. 2-3 heap
    c. 1-center problem
    d. 120-cell

9. In mathematics the _____ of a set which is equipped with the operation of addition is an element which, when added to any element x in the set, yields x. One of the most familiar additive identities is the number 0 from elementary mathematics, but additive identities occur in other mathematical structures where addition is defined, such as in groups and rings.

- The _____ familiar from elementary mathematics is zero, denoted 0. For example,

    5 + 0 = 5 = 0 + 5.

- In the natural numbers N and all of its supersets, the _____ is 0. Thus for any one of these numbers n,

    n + 0 = n = 0 + n.

Chapter 11. An Introduction to Algebra   83

Let N be a set which is closed under the operation of addition, denoted +. An _____ for N is any element e such that for any element n in N,

e + n = n = n + e.

a. Unique factorization domain
b. Additive identity
c. Unit ring
d. Algebraically independent

10. In mathematics, the term _____ has several different important meanings:

- An _____ is an equality that remains true regardless of the values of any variables that appear within it, to distinguish it from an equality which is true under more particular conditions. For this, the 'triple bar' symbol ≡ is sometimes used.
- In algebra, an _____ or _____ element of a set S with a binary operation Â· is an element e that, when combined with any element x of S, produces that same x. That is, eÂ·x = xÂ·e = x for all x in S.
  - The _____ function from a set S to itself, often denoted id or id$_S$, s the function such that i = x for all x in S. This function serves as the _____ element in the set of all functions from S to itself with respect to function composition.
  - In linear algebra, the _____ matrix of size n is the n-by-n square matrix with ones on the main diagonal and zeros elsewhere. This matrix serves as the _____ with respect to matrix multiplication.

A common example of the first meaning is the trigonometric _____

$$\sin^2 \theta + \cos^2 \theta = 1$$

which is true for all real values of θ, as opposed to

$$\cos \theta = 1,$$

which is true only for some values of θ, not all. For example, the latter equation is true when $\theta = 0$, false when $\theta = 2$

The concepts of 'additive _____' and 'multiplicative _____' are central to the Peano axioms. The number 0 is the 'additive _____' for integers, real numbers, and complex numbers. For the real numbers, for all $a \in \mathbb{R}$,

$$0 + a = a,$$

$$a + 0 = a, \text{ and}$$

$$0 + 0 = 0.$$

Similarly, The number 1 is the 'multiplicative _____' for integers, real numbers, and complex numbers.

a. Intersection
b. Action
c. ARIA
d. Identity

11. In mathematics, a _____ is a constant multiplicative factor of a certain object. For example, in the expression $9x^2$, the _____ of x^2 is 9.

The object can be such things as a variable, a vector, a function, etc.

a. Fibonacci polynomials
b. Stability radius
c. Coefficient
d. Multivariate division algorithm

12. A _____ is an algebraic equation in which each term is either a constant or the product of a constant and a single variable. _____s can have one, two, three or more variables.

_____s occur with great regularity in applied mathematics.

a. Difference of two squares
b. Quartic equation
c. Quadratic equation
d. Linear equation

Chapter 11. An Introduction to Algebra

13. In the study of metric spaces in mathematics, there are various notions of two metrics on the same underlying space being 'the same', or _____.

In the following, M will denote a non-empty set and d_1 and d_2 will denote two metrics on M.

The two metrics d_1 and d_2 are said to be topologically _____ if they generate the same topology on M.

   a. Equivalent
   b. A Mathematical Theory of Communication
   c. A chemical equation
   d. A posteriori

14. In mathematics, _____ and undefined are used to explain whether or not expressions have meaningful, sensible, and unambiguous values. Not all branches of mathematics come to the same conclusion.

The following expressions are undefined in all contexts, but remarks in the analysis section may apply.

   a. Toy model
   b. LHS
   c. Defined
   d. Plugging in

15. In mathematics, and in particular in abstract algebra, distributivity is a property of binary operations that generalises the _____ law from elementary algebra.
   a. Closure with a twist
   b. General linear group
   c. Permutation
   d. Distributive

16. _____ involves reducing the number of significant digits in a number. The result of _____ is a 'shorter' number having fewer non-zero digits yet similar in magnitude. The result is less precise but easier to use.
   a. Hyper operator
   b. Shabakh
   c. Sudan function
   d. Rounding

17. In mathematics, the multiplicative inverse of a number x, denoted 1/x or x^{-1}, is the number which, when multiplied by x, yields 1. The multiplicative inverse of x is also called the _____ of x.
    a. 120-cell
    b. 2-3 heap
    c. 1-center problem
    d. Reciprocal

ANSWER KEY

Chapter 1
1. c   2. c   3. a   4. a   5. c   6. b   7. d   8. c   9. b   10. d
11. b   12. a   13. d   14. d   15. d   16. b   17. d   18. d   19. a   20. d
21. d   22. d   23. d   24. d   25. c   26. d   27. d   28. d   29. d   30. a
31. d   32. d   33. a   34. c   35. a   36. b   37. d   38. c   39. d   40. d
41. d   42. a   43. b   44. a   45. d   46. b   47. c   48. d   49. b

Chapter 2
1. d   2. a   3. a   4. d   5. c   6. d   7. d   8. d   9. a   10. c
11. c   12. c   13. a   14. d   15. d   16. d   17. c   18. d   19. a   20. a
21. d   22. c   23. a

Chapter 3
1. d   2. d   3. c   4. d   5. c   6. c   7. d   8. d   9. d

Chapter 4
1. d   2. b   3. c   4. d   5. d   6. d   7. b   8. d   9. d   10. d
11. b   12. a   13. c   14. b   15. c   16. d   17. c   18. b   19. b   20. a
21. c   22. a

Chapter 5
1. b   2. d   3. d   4. d   5. c   6. c   7. d   8. b

Chapter 6
1. a   2. d   3. d   4. d   5. d   6. d   7. c   8. a   9. d   10. c
11. d

Chapter 7
1. b   2. d   3. d   4. a   5. d   6. c   7. d   8. d   9. d   10. d
11. d   12. d   13. c

Chapter 8
1. d   2. b   3. d   4. b   5. c   6. c   7. d   8. d   9. a   10. d
11. c   12. d   13. a   14. d   15. d   16. c   17. d   18. a   19. b   20. d
21. a   22. d   23. d   24. b   25. b   26. b   27. a   28. d   29. c   30. d
31. b   32. a   33. a   34. a   35. d   36. a   37. d   38. a   39. c   40. d
41. b

Chapter 9
1. d   2. d   3. a   4. d   5. c   6. d   7. c   8. d   9. a   10. d
11. c   12. c   13. d   14. d   15. a   16. d   17. d   18. a   19. a   20. d

Chapter 10
1. c   2. b   3. d   4. c   5. d   6. d   7. d   8. b   9. c   10. d
11. b   12. d   13. d   14. d   15. d   16. c   17. a   18. d   19. d   20. a
21. b   22. c   23. c   24. d   25. d   26. a   27. b   28. b   29. d   30. d

Chapter 11
1. d   2. d   3. b   4. a   5. a   6. a   7. c   8. a   9. b   10. d
11. c   12. d   13. a   14. c   15. d   16. d   17. d

www.ingramcontent.com/pod-product-compliance
Lightning Source LLC
Chambersburg PA
CBHW080742250426
43671CB00038B/2839